EVERYTHING
YOU NEED

EVERYTHING YOU NEED

*8 Essential Steps to a Life of Confidence
in the Promises of God*

DR. DAVID JEREMIAH

W PUBLISHING GROUP

AN IMPRINT OF THOMAS NELSON

Published in Nashville, Tennessee, by W Publishing, an imprint of Thomas Nelson.

Published in association with Yates & Yates, www.yates2.com.

Thomas Nelson titles may be purchased in bulk for educational, business, fund-raising, or sales promotional use. For information, please email SpecialMarkets@ThomasNelson.com.

Unless otherwise noted, Scripture quotations are taken from the New King James Version®. © 1982 by Thomas Nelson. Used by permission. All rights reserved.

Scripture quotations marked CSB are from the Christian Standard Bible®, Copyright © 2017 by Holman Bible Publishers. Used by permission. Christian Standard Bible® and CSB® are federally registered trademarks of Holman Bible Publishers.

Scripture quotations marked NIV are from the Holy Bible, New International Version®, NIV®. Copyright © 1973, 1978, 1984, 2011 by Biblica, Inc.® Used by permission of Zondervan. All rights reserved worldwide. www.Zondervan.com. The "NIV" and "New International Version" are trademarks registered in the United States Patent and Trademark Office by Biblica, Inc.®

Scripture quotations marked NLT are from the Holy Bible, New Living Translation. © 1996, 2004, 2007, 2013, 2015 by Tyndale House Foundation. Used by permission of Tyndale House Publishers, Inc., Carol Stream, Illinois 60188. All rights reserved.

Scripture quotations marked GNT are from the Good News Translation in Today's English Version—Second Edition. Copyright 1992 by American Bible Society. Used by permission. Italicized text is the author's emphasis added.

Any Internet addresses, phone numbers, or company or product information printed in this book are offered as a resource and are not intended in any way to be or to imply an endorsement by Thomas Nelson, nor does Thomas Nelson vouch for the existence, content, or services of these sites, phone numbers, companies, or products beyond the life of this book.

ISBN 978-0-7852-2393-1 (HC)
ISBN 978-0-7852-3115-8 (IE)

Library of Congress Control Number: 2019944263

ISBN 978-0-7852-2399-3

Printed in the United States of America

20 21 22 23 24 LSC 10 9 8 7 6 5 4 3 2 1

*To my friend Todd Durkin
and his incredible team at Fitness Quest 10*

*Your dedication to the training of the body sets a high
standard for the diligent training of the soul*

•   •   •

*For physical training is of some value,
but godliness has value for all things,
holding promise for both the present life and the life to come.*
—1 Timothy 4:8 NIV

*Dear friend, I hope all is well with you
and that you are as healthy in body
as you are strong in spirit.*
—3 John 2 NLT

CONTENTS

PROLOGUE

People often ask me, "Pastor, what's going on in the world today? What's the biggest issue we face?" I have many answers, and each contains the same overarching word—*pressure*.

Family pressure. Time pressure. Financial pressure. Unprecedented pressure to compete and succeed by society's standards—at work, in school, in our communities, and maybe even in our churches. As Christians, we're encountering pressures in our society we've never faced before. We're living in unprecedented times, which brings unparalleled tension.

But I've been encouraged recently by learning about a peculiar little fish. The Mariana snailfish lives in the deepest caverns of the ocean, where the pressure is a thousand times greater than on the surface. The temperature there is near freezing, and there's no light at those depths. But God created those fish—which are about the size of a human hand—to thrive in extreme conditions.

How do they do it? These fish possess special features such as flexible skulls and bones. They also produce distinct chemicals that stabilize their constitution, so the pressure inside them is greater than the pressure outside of them.[1]

Pretty amazing, right? God has given these strange creatures everything they need for where they are and for what He intends for them. He's given them everything they need not just to survive but to thrive.

Could that be true for you too?

Absolutely! There's a particular passage of Scripture I've studied all my life. I've known it and taught it for years. But in recent days when I, like you, have been under great pressure, it's entered my bloodstream like a transfusion.

This passage was written by someone who knew all about fish: Simon Peter. Before Jesus called him and his brother, Andrew, saying, "Follow Me, and I will make you fishers of men" (Matt. 4:19), Simon Peter ran a fishing business in Galilee.

After a remarkable three years with Jesus, as recounted in the Gospels, Peter went on to help establish the early church, chronicled in the book of Acts. In spite of the constant threat of persecution, he devoted the rest of his life to extending the kingdom of God. He spent his last days in prison awaiting execution, yet even then the joy within him was greater than the fear around him. He had everything he needed to maintain his faith, optimism, and effectiveness for Jesus—until the very moment he entered heaven.

Peter's last letter was written to "those who through the righteousness of our God and Savior Jesus Christ have received a faith as precious as ours" (2 Peter 1:1 NIV).

What does that mean? It means your experience with Jesus can be as precious to you as Peter's was to him. That's remarkable to consider. And in the verses that follow, he explained how. This is the passage that gripped my heart so powerfully in recent months that it led me to write this book:

His divine power has given to us all things that pertain to life and godliness, through the knowledge of Him who called us by glory and virtue, by which have been given to us exceedingly great and precious promises, that through these you may be partakers of the divine nature, having escaped the corruption that is in the world through lust. But also for this very reason, giving all diligence, add to your faith virtue, to virtue knowledge, to knowledge self-control, to self-control perseverance, to perseverance godliness, to godliness brotherly kindness, and to brotherly kindness love. For if these things are yours and abound, you will be neither barren nor unfruitful in the knowledge of our Lord Jesus Christ. For he who lacks these things is shortsighted, even to blindness, and has forgotten that he was cleansed from his old sins. Therefore, brethren, be even more diligent to make your call and election sure, for if you do these things you will never stumble; for so an entrance will be supplied to you abundantly into the everlasting kingdom of our Lord and Savior Jesus Christ. (vv. 3–11)

In *Everything You Need: 8 Essential Steps to a Life of Confidence in the Promises of God*, I'll follow the trail of God's logic that runs through the passage like a needle pulling a golden thread. I'll show you how God's divine power gives you everything you need—not half, or most, or a whole lot of what you need. He has given you *everything* you need to develop a godly life!

That's just the beginning. God has also devised an ingenious way of conveying His power right into the center of your soul through the live wires of His biblical promises, or—as Peter called them—His great and precious promises. These promises energize you and enable you to share His divine nature. In this book we explore how you can receive that energy.

I'll also show you the eight essential steps Peter listed—each building on the other, and every one essential for a life of courage, confidence, and effectiveness. Here's a preview of the amazing character qualities we'll explore together in these pages:

- Diligence—the pursuit of the Lord with all your heart.
- Virtue—the sustaining joy of a God-pleasing life.
- Knowledge—accelerated growth and wisdom that come from knowing God better.
- Self-Control—the skill of bringing your habits under the Holy Spirit's control.
- Perseverance—resilience that casts off disappointment and discouragement.
- Godliness—the mirror image of Christ in your personality.
- Brotherly Kindness—friendliness that draws people to yourself and to Jesus.
- Love—the essence of serving God and others.

In the final chapter I'll explain how God will bless and use you in truly unimaginable ways as you put these virtues into practice.

Peter wrote, "If these things are yours and abound, you will be neither barren nor unfruitful in the knowledge of our Lord Jesus Christ" (2 Peter 1:8). This is one of God's great understatements! If these virtues are yours and if they abound in your life—meaning if you embrace them and fill your heart with them—there's no limit to what you can achieve. And there's no pressure you can't withstand.

These eight qualities are indispensable today. Think of them as tools in your backpack for your adventure of hiking through life. The Old Testament prophet Habakkuk said, "The LORD God is my strength; He will make my feet like deer's feet, and He will make me walk on my high hills" (Hab. 3:19).

If God can equip a small fish in the deepest sea to withstand the pressure it's under, and if He can keep a single deer surefooted on the summits, then He's got you covered.

It's time to unpack all God has given you and commit to cultivating the strength of character you'll need to face the pressures in this world.

Once you master these precious verses of the Bible—or rather, once they master you—you'll realize you have everything you need!

Even more, you'll find He *is* everything you need.

I don't want to pressure you, but what are you waiting for? Is life getting easier? No? Then read on, and let's get started!

Chapter 1

THE PROMISE

The Pacific Crest Trail is one of the most beautiful but demanding hikes in the world—2,650 miles from Mexico to Canada. It runs through California, Oregon, and Washington, winding through desert wastelands, along breathtaking ridges, and beside glaciated expanses.

In 2018, Katharina Groene traveled from Germany to experience the PCT for herself. She made it northbound over two thousand miles, all the way to Washington State. For a couple of hours on October 22, she fell in with Nancy Abell of Seattle. As they parted, Nancy, a lifelong local hiker, worried about Katharina. The German didn't have snowshoes and wasn't prepared for the next leg of the trip, which negotiated Glacier Peak. Nancy tried to dissuade Katharina from continuing, but to no avail. Katharina was five months into her trip. She wasn't about to quit.

Katharina soon regretted her decision. When conditions turned deadly, she realized she didn't have everything she needed for the elements. Her clothing was soaked, and her shoes were no match for the snow and ice. She became dehydrated and hungry, with only a Pop-Tart left in her pack. One of her two tarps blew away, and she lost two pairs of gloves. Frostbite set in. She had no phone service.

Soon, Katharina came to believe she would perish in the wilds of the North Cascades. She even started composing goodbye messages to her loved ones.

Then she heard a sound through the biting wind: blades chopping the air. A rescue helicopter appeared—a HAWK1 from Snohomish, flying low and sweeping just under the heavy clouds. The pilots had their heads out, following Katharina's tracks in the snow until they finally spotted her in her red jacket near a stand of old timber.

How did the rescue team know to look for her? How did they find her?

The credit goes to Nancy Abell, who couldn't stop thinking about her new friend. Seeing the storm blowing in, she instinctively knew Katharina was in trouble. Nancy notified the authorities, and the search was on. Katharina was saved.[1]

Like a hiker in the wild, we sometimes find ourselves stranded and isolated, caught in an unexpected storm, even endangered by life's circumstances. It's dangerous to be ill-equipped for the journey. When we haven't packed the right gear, we're underprepared, overexposed, and at risk of the elements.

That is never God's plan for us. Like a divine Outfitter, He wants to give us everything we need for the journey. He knows how to equip us to be people of character, able to face the ruggedness of the world with dignity and strength. He furnishes all we need for every condition. But we've got to turn from our meager resources and embrace the abundant ones He provides.

In this chapter, I want to share with you a specific Scripture from the writings of Simon Peter. I believe it will encourage you for the rest of your life. No matter what you face, this passage will strip away all your excuses for floundering and flailing. It will boost your confidence and enable you to make the most of each day, week, and year, whatever the weather of life.

You'll find it in 2 Peter 1:3–4. As you read this passage, don't skim over the verses. Listen to each word as if God were speaking just to you.

His divine power has given to us all things that pertain to life and godliness, through the knowledge of Him who called us by glory and virtue, by which have been given to us exceedingly great and precious promises, that through these you may be partakers of the divine nature, having escaped the corruption that is in the world through lust.

According to Peter, who literally walked beside Jesus, you have been given everything you need for life and godliness. Not some things you need, not many things, not even most things, but *everything*. Believe it or not, God has already provided the resources you need to successfully navigate life with confidence and grace.

So what specifically are those resources? It starts with access to His power.

YOU HAVE GOD'S POWER

Have you ever experienced a spiritual power outage? For many, it's going to the doctor and hearing bad news. It's going to work and learning you've been laid off. It's answering the phone call that says your child is in trouble. It's watching the stock market plunge as you're about to retire. These things and more are bound to happen to you and me, for we have many troubles in this world.

That's why Peter began his letter by telling us about God's almighty power. It's His power that enables us to overcome the trials of life—to live the life for which we were created. If that feels big and inspiring, well . . . it is!

Verse 3 says, "His divine power has given to us all things that pertain to life and godliness." What is godliness? What does it mean to live a godly life?

Godliness encompasses behaviors, words, and attitudes that reflect what God would do on earth if He were to come down as a person—as He did during the incarnation of Jesus Christ. A godly life manifests the purity and purpose of God from the inside out. It's literally a matter of Christ living His life through us consistently by means of the indwelling Holy Spirit.

Godliness may seem too lofty a goal to attempt. And it is—if you attempt it in your own power. But Peter was pointing you toward a power that will enable you to live a godly life. What kind of power can do that?

IT'S UNLIMITED POWER

Is the sun shining outside your window today? I hope so, because I want you to consider the incredible power of solar energy. Our sun is a blinding star, so huge that about one million earths could fit inside it. It takes only eight minutes for a beam of light and heat to travel ninety-three million miles from the sun to the earth, and it arrives right on schedule and in the exact proportion needed to sustain life on our planet.

The temperature at the surface of the sun is about ten thousand degrees Fahrenheit. The temperature at its core may reach twenty-seven million degrees. The sun never shuts down, though it may occasionally flare up. Essentially, it's a gaseous ball of continuously occurring nuclear explosions, radiating energy uniformly in all directions throughout the solar system.

Every second the sun produces enough energy to power human civilization for almost five hundred thousand years. Imagine if we could collect and use all that energy! And that's only one second of its power. The sun has enough nuclear fuel to burn for another five billion years.[2]

Yet the sun is only one medium-size star in a universe filled with trillions of others. Astronomers estimate there are one hundred billion to four hundred billion stars in our galaxy. And images from the Hubble Space Telescope suggest there may be two trillion other galaxies in the universe!

Think of all the energy radiating from all those stars and ask yourself, "What source of power could so animate the universe? Where did all this energy come from?"

It comes from God. His power can light up the universe, fire up the stars, power the planets, move the oceans in their undulating tides, and give life to every creature on earth without being diminished by one kilowatt.

Since God has all the power in the universe at His command, God can do anything He chooses. And here is the incredible truth that should shake you to the core whenever you feel unequipped to handle what life throws at you: God has chosen to give you access to the greatness of His power.

The word *power* was in the vocabulary of nearly every Old and New Testament writer. If you go through the Scripture highlighting this word, you'll run out of yellow ink.

The Bible says, "Power belongs to God. . . . Yours, O Lord, is the greatness, the power and the glory, the victory and the majesty; for all that is in heaven and in earth is Yours" (Ps. 62:11; 1 Chron. 29:11).

Consider Paul's prayer for the Ephesians: "[I pray] . . . that you may know . . . the exceeding greatness of His power toward us who believe, according to the working of His mighty power which He worked in Christ when He raised Him from the dead and seated Him at His right hand in the heavenly places" (Eph. 1:18–20).

Paul used the word *dunamis* to refer to God's power toward us, the word from which we get *dynamite*. Dynamite can do many things, but it can't raise the dead. But that's what the power of God did in the resurrection of Christ. And that's the power of God that resides in you.

God's power is unlimited. Human power gives out, and we ourselves become weary. But the Bible says those who wait upon the Lord will renew their strength (Isa. 40:31).

If you're a follower of the Son who shines in all His brilliance, then you're never powerless. There is no problem or situation in life for which God's mighty power, given to you, is not adequate.

IT'S UNLEASHED POWER

When you trust Jesus Christ as your Savior, the power of God Almighty is unleashed in your life. Think what would happen if every follower of Jesus stopped looking everywhere else for this power and instead focused on what God has already given them. That's God's desire.

His divine power has given us all things. What a phrase—*all things*! Jesus said, "With God *all things* are possible" (Matt. 19:26). And Romans 8:28 says, "We know that *all things* work together for good to those who love God, to those who are the called according to His purpose."

And here's my all-time favorite "all things" verse. This verse has more superlatives in it than any other verse in the Bible: "God is able to make *all* grace *abound* toward you, that you, *always* having *all* sufficiency in *all things*, may have an *abundance* for *every* good work" (2 Cor. 9:8).

Do you need joy—a heart of holy happiness that comes from Christ and keeps us buoyant in life? It's available.

Do you need help discarding shame and guilt? His power, applied to your life by the blood of Jesus Christ, is the world's greatest cleansing agent.

Do you need wisdom to deal with your problems? Christ is both the "power of God and the wisdom of God" (1 Cor. 1:24). He will guide you through the trails and trials of life.

Do you need enough energy to fulfill God's work and will for your life day by day? The Bible says we're "strengthened with all might, according to His glorious power, for all patience and longsuffering with joy" (Col. 1:11).

Put simply, you *can* "do all things through Christ who strengthens" you! (Phil. 4:13).

IT'S UNLOCKED POWER

God's power is unlimited because it's divine power that energizes you to live a godly Jesus-life on earth. But there's another aspect of God's power that meets your needs. This power is unlocked through your "knowledge of Him who called us by glory and virtue" (2 Peter 1:3).

Francis Bacon, the sixteenth-century statesman and amateur scientist, had an insatiable curiosity. Educated by Puritans, he once stated he had three goals in life: to uncover truth, to serve his country, and to serve his church. He's credited with developing the scientific method and helping unleash the scientific revolution.

Bacon is also credited with the phrase, "Knowledge is power." But that's not exactly what he said. In his book *Sacred Meditations*, Bacon actually wrote, "Knowledge is His Power."[3] Francis Bacon understood that wisdom and knowledge lead to strength and success—when they find their source in God.

Centuries earlier, another statesman and philosopher named Solomon wrote, "A wise man is strong, yes, a man of knowledge increases strength" (Prov. 24:5).

But I like the way Peter put it best: "By his divine power, God has given us everything we need for living a godly life. We have received all of this by coming to know him" (2 Peter 1:3 NLT).

When Peter talked about the knowledge of Him who called us, he had three things in mind:

1. We must know Jesus personally. It's one thing to know about someone; it's another thing to know someone personally.
2. We need to grow in our knowledge of Scripture and the doctrines, truths, and realities of God.

3. And we must grow in our knowledge of His patterns for our lives. This means integrating our knowledge of Him with our lives.

When you have a personal connection with Jesus Christ, and when you walk with Him and get to know Him better each day—which includes studying His Word with a sense of listening to His voice and meeting with Him in prayer—you grow in your relationship with Him. Through the years you grow closer, wiser, and stronger in Christ.

Donna and I have been married fifty-six years. We fell in love before our wedding, but it was not as mature a love as it is now. Through the years we've gotten to know each other better, and our lives have been fused together with the kind of love that only comes by facing the difficulties of life and maturing as a couple. That's akin to what Peter was saying. As we come to know Jesus better—growing in His Word, growing in prayer, growing in faith—His unlimited power is unlocked and unleashed in us.

Have you ever had the frustrating experience of charging your phone only to realize hours later the cord wasn't plugged into the wall? It can be maddening—all that time wasted and still no power.

In a similar way, if you're not experiencing the power of God in your life, check your connections—you might not be plugged into the right energy source. God's endless energy and omnipotent power radiate from His Word. If you feel overwhelmed with life, immerse yourself in the Scriptures. Spend time with God in prayer. And let His power lift you, sustain you, and strengthen you as He has promised.

YOU HAVE GOD'S PROMISES

In verse 4, Peter went on to tell us that God's power is communicated to us through His promises, and it's His promises that sustain our faith. What does that mean? How can a promise sustain anything?

Robert "R. G." Williams lived with his family—his mother and nine older siblings—in poverty in a rough part of Louisville, Kentucky. As a boy he took the bus to school. From his window on the bus each morning, R. G. saw drug addicts, homeless people, and alcoholics buying their liquor and cigarettes. But inside the bus there was a redeeming presence: his bus driver, Louise Garnett, "a very motherly type." R. G. sat where he could talk with her, and she always asked about his grades and schoolwork and if he'd been eating.

R. G.'s mother became ill, and at age thirteen, he decided to take matters into his own hands. He thought he would become a bus driver himself to help his family with their bills. Using some of his church clothes, he sewed himself a bus uniform. He took one of the caps his dad had left behind, and he made himself a badge out of cardboard and aluminum foil.

Then R. G. went down to the bus depot, saw an empty bus, sat in the driver's seat, and started the engine. Telling himself, "I need to do this for my family," the first-time bus driver pulled out of the parking lot and clipped the mirror of a nearby truck. Feeling panicked, R. G. floored the gas pedal and started going about forty-five miles per hour down the street. The police took off after him, sirens piercing the air. But R. G. was too afraid to stop. He kept to his route. Finally, police set up a roadblock and stopped the bus.

At his trial R. G. was given a chance to explain his situation, and the court was sympathetic. The Transit Authority of River City made an astounding promise. As R. G. recalled, "[They told me] that if I kept my nose clean, I could come back for a job when I was twenty-five. At thirteen, I was thinking, 'There is hope!'"

R. G. grew up, graduated from high school, and joined the navy to train as a cryptologist. But when he turned twenty-five, he left the navy, returned to Louisville, and asked for his promised job. And he got it![4]

That promise, made in a Louisville courtroom, stayed with a boy for more than a decade—guiding him, sustaining him, and giving him hope. How much more do the promises of God sustain us! The Lord transmits His power into our lives by His exceedingly great and precious promises.

Speaking generally, these promises are great because they come from a great God and they lead to a great life. But we can go deeper in our understanding because these promises are great for at least three additional reasons.

GOD'S PROMISES ARE INCALCULABLE

God's promises are exceedingly great because they're incalculable. No one can fully count the number of promises God placed in the Bible, although Dr. Everek R. Storms of Ontario decided to try.

"All my life," he said, "I have seen various figures quoted as to the number of promises in the Bible. The one most generally given is 30,000. Since this is a round number, I have always been a little suspicious about it. Furthermore, since there are only 31,101 verses in the Bible, it would mean that there would be practically one promise in every verse."

That inspired Dr. Storms to conduct his own study. According to Storms's calculations, there are a grand total of 8,810 promises in the Bible. About 85 percent of them are made by God to human beings. Only one book of the Bible contains no promise at all: Titus. Isaiah contains more than one thousand promises. What section of Scripture most impressed Storms? "The most outstanding chapter as far as promises are concerned is Psalm 37," he wrote. "Practically every verse is a most wonderful promise."[5]

But with all due respect to Dr. Storms, it gets better. Many verses in the Bible may not be written in the form of a promise—and yet they are promises.

For example, think of 2 Corinthians 1:18, which says, "God is faithful." That isn't technically a promise; it's a statement of fact. But, oh, the promise implied by that truth! If God is faithful, then He will be faithful to you. You can read that as a promise!

The prayers of the Bible are implicit promises. When Jesus taught us to pray, "Give us this day our daily bread" (Matt. 6:11), He understood God can and will do that in answer to our sincere prayers.

Even the commands of the Bible are promises turned inside out. When Paul wrote, "Rejoice always" in 1 Thessalonians 5:16, he was issuing instruction, but only God can empower us to keep that command. You could paraphrase that verse to say, "Trust God, for He will enable you to rejoice in all situations."

So how in the world can you count the promises of God? You cannot! His promises are incalculable because the entire Bible is a virtual vault filled with infinite riches issued to you through every single verse. Somewhere in every single verse, explicit or implicit, is a promise.

GOD'S PROMISES ARE INFALLIBLE

Second, God's promises are great because they're infallible. The Bible says, "For every one of God's promises is 'Yes' in [Christ]. Therefore, through him we also say 'Amen' to the glory of God" (2 Cor. 1:20 CSB).

In other words, "Lord, have You promised to never leave us or forsake us and to work all things for our good?" He says, *Yes!* and we say, "Amen—so be it!"

"Have You promised to hear and answer our prayers? To watch over us and deliver us from evil? To give peace and strength as needed?" He says, *Yes!* and we say, "Amen!"

"Have You promised us an eternal home in heaven, where sin, sickness, and sorrow can never intrude?" He says, *Yes!* and we say, "Amen!"

That equation works for all God's promises. For no matter how many promises God has made, they are all yes in Christ, and through us is the *amen* for the glory of God.[6]

Thomas Bragg and Eddie Lama served in the same platoon in Vietnam with the army's First Cavalry Division; they were buddies from the start. Thomas was "a twenty-year-old short, brash black man" and Eddie was "a twenty-year-old curly haired, freckled white man." They bonded quickly during the conflict and promised to stay in touch and visit each other after the war. But Eddie Lama didn't make it home. While covering for an American helicopter and trying to fend off enemy snipers, he was struck in the head by a bullet and killed instantly. Eddie was evacuated from the battlefield, and Thomas never had a chance to say goodbye.

Thomas returned home with a sense of loss and pain. He kept a trove of photographs in a cigar box, and over the years he'd pull them out to remember his friendship with Eddie. The pain was always there, but Thomas went on with his life as the decades passed. One day Thomas realized he should keep the promise he made to Eddie to visit him after the war. He began trying to locate Eddie's grave but had no contacts, no phone numbers, no people to ask. Finally, he found Michael Lund, professor emeritus at Longwood University, who led a writing program for veterans. After some research, they located Eddie's gravesite.

Thomas drove from his home in Blackstone, Virginia, to a cemetery in Mundelein, Illinois. Exactly fifty years from the day his army buddy and best friend Eddie was killed, Thomas Bragg stood over Eddie's grave and had a very emotional visit. A journalist who recorded the story said the moment was powerful because it was the story of a man keeping his promise.[7]

That was one man and one promise kept. Now imagine almighty God making a promise to you. You know without doubt He will keep it. The Bible teaches that God keeps every promise He has ever made, and He keeps them fully, totally, in detail, and forever. His Word cannot be broken. That's why His promises are described as exceedingly powerful, because they exceed anything we can compare them to!

GOD'S PROMISES ARE AVAILABLE

That leads me to the third reason His promises are exceedingly great: they're not only incalculable and infallible; they're available. No matter how powerful something is, it's worthless if it isn't available. Without the endless treasure of God's promises available to us, we have no assurance about anything: no hope, no security, no safety, no encouragement, and no comfort. But God has given us His Word. His promises provide an endless supply of grace for us every day.

Precious was an important word to Peter. He used it eight times in his two letters. But when Peter used the word to describe God's promises, he didn't mean it in a sentimental way, as in "Oh, how precious!" He didn't mean "sweet," as in adorable babies, kittens, and teddy bears. He was using the word in its truer meaning: something rare and infinitely valuable. Think precious stones and metals. Think gold.

Gold is a unique precious metal. God made it and caused it to be buried in the earth, and He values it so much He used it for paving material in New Jerusalem. Experts say it has special chemical properties. Sure, silver has more industrial uses than gold. And copper is more useful for its electrical conductivity. But gold has a special chemical composition that cannot be destroyed by water, time, or fire. It is malleable (it spreads without cracking); it is ductile (it stretches without breaking); it is rare (all the gold ever mined would only fill two Olympic swimming pools); and of course it is beautiful.[8]

Gold is a precious metal in the way that Peter used the word *precious*. Each and every promise God issues to you in His Word is precious in this sense, so valuable that just one of His promises makes you infinitely richer than one who owns all the gold in both those swimming pools!

You are the recipient of these precious promises. To fully embrace what that means, you must know what it is you have. As you read this book, you'll understand and recognize the life-changing gifts God has given you. Only when you understand these gifts, and how to use them, can you comprehend how well-equipped and abundantly prepared for life you are. You have everything you need!

William Randolph Hearst was a wealthy twentieth-century newspaper publisher and an avid art collector. One day he read a description of some valuable pieces of art, and he decided he had to have them. Immediately Hearst commissioned his agent to find those pieces and add them to his collection, regardless of cost. You can imagine his surprise when he received a telegram from his art agent telling him the pieces had been located—they were in Hearst's own warehouse where his collection of art was stored![9]

If William Randolph Hearst had compared the valuable items he impulsively wanted with the precious items he already possessed, he'd have discovered that the very things he longed for were already his.

It's that way with the promises of God. Whatever you need is already stored away in the vault of Scripture, and you can open it with the key of faith. All the promises of God are available to enrich you and to meet all your needs.

YOU HAVE GOD'S PURPOSE

Why does God provide you with His divine power through His promises? Because He wants to accomplish something in your life. He has a purpose in mind for you. Follow Peter's logic: "His divine power has given us everything we need for a godly life . . . that through them you may participate in the divine nature, having escaped the corruption in the world caused by evil desires" (2 Peter 1:3–4 NIV).

God has a purpose for you: to partake in His divine nature! That doesn't mean you're going to be God Himself. Only God is God, and living a godly life doesn't turn us into little gods. What it means is that His divine power transmitted through His precious promises can make you more *like* Him. He wants to infuse your personality with more of His joy, His patience, His wisdom, His influence, and His priorities.

At the same time, another process will occur in your life: you'll have a greater ability to say no to the corruption in the world that comes through evil desires.

Imagine you draw a graph of your life based on this remarkable passage. The graph has two trend lines. The first line, hopefully ascending, plots your growth in godliness. The second line, hopefully descending, shows the opposite; we'll call it spiritual immaturity.

The more you lean on the power and promises of God throughout your life, the more these lines diverge. The godly line goes up, showing your increasing spiritual maturity. When it does, the ungodly line has to go down.

Put simply, your goal is this: more like Jesus, less like the world.

Have you ever heard that married couples who live together long enough start to look alike? This isn't a myth. Scientists say the emotional interactions within a marriage, a couple's diet and environment, and their hobbies and exercise all can create similar complexions. Plus, partners tend to imitate each other's habits and body language. According to University of Michigan psychologist Robert Zajonc, the happier a couple is, the more likely they are to have increased physical similarity.[10]

It's the same in our relationship with God. When we spend time with God through Jesus Christ, drawing from His power and living by His promises, He fulfills His purpose in us bit by bit, making us more and more like our Savior. Through His grace, we become "conformed to the image of His Son" (Rom. 8:29).

DOWNLOADING GOD'S POWER

God's power, God's promises, God's purpose—these are a legacy of truth for every believer. But how do you download this power into your life?

What practical steps can you take to personalize what you've read about in this chapter?

Here's a simple five-step strategy I've found helpful: analyze, personalize, memorize, verbalize, and organize.

ANALYZE

Take inventory. Where do you need the most help in your spiritual life? What do you struggle with? What are your most difficult challenges? Where are you frustrated and not doing what you intend to do spiritually? What's keeping you from enjoying a life of godliness and joy on your Christian journey?

All of us, no matter how long we've followed Christ, have what the Bible calls "besetting sins."[11] Even the great apostle Paul had his struggles. This is how he described it in his letter to the Romans: "For what I will to do, that I do not practice, but what I hate, that I do. . . . For the good that I will to do, I do not, but the evil I will not to do, that I practice. . . . O wretched man that I am! Who will deliver me?" (7:15, 19, 24).

So, in this first step, take honest inventory of your life. This is between you and God, and it will help you immensely to write out what you discover. No one else needs to see it, but you'll achieve great clarity in this process if you review your recent days and make a list of things that most concern you about your life and godliness. Don't go crazy; just identify five things that bother you most.

PERSONALIZE

Now that you have your list, start finding the powerful promises of God's Word that deal with your challenges. Build a customized treasure of verses that speak to each of the issues you're facing. If you've never done anything like this before, get a good concordance and look up the key words on your list. You can use a written concordance or do this on the computer.

Many verses you locate won't speak directly to your need, but some will. Write those down, and keep adding verses that speak to your heart. You may only find one or two verses the first week. But that's more than you had when you started! Remember, these precious promises convey God's power directly into your life.

As you read the Bible more deeply and more often, verses you've read before but never really noticed will jump out at you. These will be some of the most powerful messages you'll ever get from God. So stop! Thank God for His promises, and immediately write those verses in your journal.

Slowly but surely you'll build a power source that will serve you every day for the rest of your life. Guard this list with your life! Make copies regularly so the enemy can never take your great and precious promises away. They belong to you alone. There is no one like you, so there will never be another list of Scriptures like yours. You are the object of God's personal love, and His Word will never let you forget that.

And remember, the Bible book with the most promises is Isaiah, and the chapter with the most promises is Psalm 37.

MEMORIZE

There is tremendous value in memorizing Scripture because it's a transformational discipline—it changes us. David understood this value, which is why he wrote, "Your word I have hidden in my heart, that I might not sin against You" (Ps. 119:11).

I started memorizing the Bible as a child as part of the Bible Memory Association. All these years later, I still remember verses I memorized back then. There are many strategies for memorizing God's Word, but the one I like best is to create three-by-five-inch cards, writing the Scripture reference on one side and the words to the verse on the other. Periodically throughout the day, prompt yourself by reading one side of the card and trying to recall the content of the other side. If you don't want to carry your cards, consider downloading a Bible memory app to your phone.

The reasons for Bible memorization are many. For now, concentrate on one: when you memorize verses from the Bible, God's promises never leave you. Most of the time when we need one of God's amazing promises, we're not in church or we don't have a Bible handy. But when you memorize the important verses on your list, you can recall the appropriate promise anywhere, at any time.

VERBALIZE

Now, to cement these promises in your heart and mind, speak them out loud. Share them with your spouse or a close friend. Find every opportunity you can to say these promises audibly. Say them aloud and address your problem with them.

Remember, it's one thing to tell God about your problems, but sometimes you need to tell your problems about God. In other words, you need to talk to yourself and let your problems know they're no match for the promises of God.

ORGANIZE

As you accumulate promises, you'll want to organize them. I suggest you find a small journal or notebook and give each page a title. (Hint: If you use a loose-leaf notebook, you can keep the pages in alphabetical order as you add new passages.) The title of each page is the problem or difficulty for which you have collected your promises. Write or type the problem in the upper right-hand corner of the paper and organize them alphabetically. You're building your own custom book of promises.

 ## WHO WOULD GIVE ME A GIFT LIKE THAT?

At age two, Kaden Koebcke had kidney failure. By the time he reached sixth grade, his condition was seriously deteriorating.

Kaden had endured a kidney transplant when he was five. His

father donated that kidney, but complications required it to be removed days later. The boy had been on dialysis ever since, with a dialysis/plasmapheresis catheter implanted in his small chest. Doctors told his parents that because of his condition, he couldn't receive a kidney from a deceased donor. He needed a living kidney donor. Desperate, his family sought help through a Facebook page called Kaden's Kidney Search.

Meanwhile, Kaden's sixth-grade technology teacher, Will Wilkinson, was profoundly touched by his ailing student. Will quietly decided to find out if he was a match and, if he was, to give Kaden one of his kidneys. Will was a match, and he became Kaden's kidney donor.

It wasn't until Will came to visit after his own recovery that Kaden and his family learned who the donor was. Kaden's parents struggled to find words to express their gratitude to the man who literally gave their son a chance at a normal life.

"The Wilkinsons moved to the Atlanta area almost the same time as we did," Kaden's mother wrote. "We both chose the same school for our kids. Our sons are in the same class. We have been blessed to call them our friends. This all isn't coincidence.

"God had a hand in all of this. He places us where we need to be, and puts people in our lives that we need. Will, you are such a selfless person, our true hero . . . We love you, we appreciate you, and we just cannot thank you enough."[12]

Pause for a moment and put yourself in Kaden's place.

Is it hard for you to imagine someone loving you enough to do something like Will Wilkinson did? Probably. But it shouldn't be, because Someone already did. Someone already gave you everything you need for a second chance at the life God planned for you. He did it out of love and at great sacrifice to Himself.

So how will you spend the life that was given to you at great sacrifice? The choice is yours. You can live it in a godly way—or not. You see, according to 2 Peter, you have everything you need to live in a way that will make your life-saving Donor proud.

I began this chapter by describing a woman who was ill-equipped for the journey she faced. As a disciple of Jesus, that need never be true of you. Instead, God Himself has equipped you. God Himself has stuffed your backpack to the brim with everything you will ever need not just to survive your journey but to thrive along the way!

Indeed, when the power of God is unleashed in your life, it enables you, as Habakkuk 3:19 says, "to tread on the heights" (NIV). As His power is transmitted to you through His very great and precious promises, you are increasingly transformed according to His purposes. You become more like Him and less like the world.

What power! What promises! What a purpose! I want to tell you with all my heart—you have a God who gives you everything you need because He Himself is everything you need.

He who did not spare His own Son, but delivered Him up for us
all, how shall He not with Him also freely give us all things?

—ROMANS 8:32

Chapter 2

MUSCULAR FAITH

Whatever your political views, if you watched the televised funeral of President George H. W. Bush, you probably wiped a tear from your eyes when his son, George W. Bush, gripped the pulpit, bent over choked in grief, and called his dad "a great and noble man, and the best father a son or daughter could have."

That poignant moment occurred near the end of Bush's eulogy of his father, and as I listened to the tribute I was particularly struck by one statement. The younger Bush said of his father, "He taught us that a day was not meant to be wasted. He played golf at a legendary pace. I always wondered why he insisted on speed golf. He was a good golfer. Well, here's my conclusion: He played fast so that he could move on to the next event, to enjoy the rest of the day, to expend his enormous energy, to live it all. He was born with just two settings: full throttle, then sleep."[1]

I believe the apostle Peter was a "full throttle" guy too. His adrenaline never seemed to run out, and he encouraged his readers to be fully engaged in their pursuit of Christ and the Christlike life.

In 2 Peter 1:5, the apostle used a word frequently found in the Bible—*diligence*. Diligence may sound old-fashioned, but it's a quality I keep bumping into. It's especially present in biographies of productive, effective men and women past and present, some well-known and others who lived under the radar.

One of my better-known heroes is Charles Haddon Spurgeon. I've probably quoted him in books and sermons more than any other single figure. In 1850, Spurgeon, in his mid-teens at the time, decided to follow Jesus Christ. He started preaching the very next year, and there was no stopping him. At age nineteen, he became pastor of the New Park Street Chapel in London, and almost instantly no auditorium in London was large enough for the crowds wanting to hear him. With few or no notes, he stood in the pulpit and eloquently expounded the Word of God.

Stenographers in the audience recorded his sermons in shorthand, and he personally edited each one for publication. By the end of his life, the collected volumes of Spurgeon's sermons represented the largest single set of Christian books by one author in the history of Christianity—a feat that stands to this day. His 3,561 sermons are bound in sixty-three volumes filled with twenty million words—the equivalent of the twenty-seven volumes of the *Encyclopedia Britannica*.

Spurgeon himself was a ravenous reader. His personal library contained twelve thousand volumes, and he typically read six books a week. He devoured commentaries and works by the Puritan giants, as well as newspapers and periodicals. His Bible was always open and his pen always flowing. He answered correspondence, started dozens of benevolent agencies, published a magazine called *The Sword and the Trowel*, established a college where he lectured, and wrote one book after another on many subjects. He often worked eighteen hours a day and preached ten times a week.[2]

Spurgeon had only two speeds: full throttle and sleep. He once said,

"A man cannot be idle and yet have Christ's sweet company. Christ is a quick walker and when His people would talk with Him they must travel quickly, too, or else they will soon lose His company."[3]

On another occasion Spurgeon exclaimed, "The sin of doing nothing is about the biggest of all sins, for it involves most of the others. . . . Horrible idleness! God save us from it!"[4]

Two men. One was a president, the other a preacher—but they both shared a common virtue: diligence. And they both changed the world.

Let's face it: we don't get very far if we idle through life. When your car is idling, it's making no progress toward the destination. And when you're idling, you're wasting one resource that is not recoverable—your time, the very hours of your life.

UNDERSTANDING THE HEART OF DILIGENCE

According to the book of 2 Peter, diligence is an essential ingredient in withstanding the pressures of the world and grasping everything you need for life and godliness. The Lord offers divine resources to us through His very great and precious promises, but you have to grab on to the promises and go with them.

If you're going to experience true transformation of character and have the personal capacity to wholly follow Christ, you have to understand diligence. That's what 2 Peter 1:5 is all about.

THE MEANING OF DILIGENCE

What do I mean, then, by the word *diligence*? The term used by the New Testament authors meant "to make every effort; to act with urgency, zeal, and earnestness."[5] It pictured the kind of effort a runner makes when she's approaching the finish line and, finding a new burst of energy, gives it all she has until she breaks the tape.

Our modern *Merriam-Webster* dictionary says diligence is "steady, earnest, and energetic effort."[6]

The original author of that dictionary, Noah Webster, was himself a dedicated Christian who published his magnum opus in 1806. Webster was known for his diligence, working day and night for many years to produce his world-famous work in which he defined seventy thousand words and helped shape American English. His original definition of the word *diligence* is still the best I've found: "Steady in application to business; constant in effort or exertion to accomplish what is undertaken; assiduous; attentive; industrious; not idle or negligent."[7]

The Old Testament book of Proverbs helps us understand the true meaning of diligence when it goes out of its way to contrast diligence with laziness. Diligence is the opposite of laziness:

- "The hand of the diligent will rule, but the lazy man will be put to forced labor" (12:24).
- "The soul of a lazy man desires, and has nothing; but the soul of the diligent shall be made rich" (13:4).

New Testament scholar Andreas Köstenberger reminds us that this virtue is never easy and is often at odds with our culture:

Diligence is hard. It is tough. It is far easier to slack off, take an easier road, follow shortcuts, or simply give up. Diligence is particularly difficult in our fast-food, microwave culture. As Americans, we don't want to have to wait for results or labor and toil for future gain in the absence of immediate gratification. We want the maximum payoff for the smallest possible amount of labor.[8]

And yet I don't want you to mistake *diligence* for *workaholism*. Diligent people do tend to work hard, of course, but Peter wasn't talking about obsessively working. He was exhorting us to diligently follow Christ, going full throttle in our pursuit of the godly life and working harder to be better—to be more like Christ.

Until now in the passage, Peter had been telling us about God's resources, His sufficiency, His great and precious promises, and His desire for us to live above the ways of the world. But now there's a shift in the text. This kind of life doesn't happen to people whose lives are on automatic pilot, Peter explained. It requires effort. It requires diligence.

Verse 5 says, "Giving all diligence, add to your faith." Not just diligence, but *all* diligence!

As one scholar noted, "The words *giving all diligence* could also be translated 'with intense effort.' This suggests the seriousness and importance of our responsibility. We cannot expect to grow and abound in the 'precious faith' without zealous endeavor."[9]

Terry Fator is the best-known ventriloquist in the world. He achieved stardom on *America's Got Talent*, and since then he's been a marquee personality in Las Vegas. But many people don't know how hard Fator worked for thirty years before anyone knew about him. A journalist called it "thirty years of diligent work."

When Fator was only ten, he found a book about ventriloquism in his school library. He read it and was hooked. He bought an inexpensive puppet and practiced for hours every day, sometimes "performing in front of church groups and at talent shows." After three decades of hardworking, persevering practice, Fator hit the big time. He is said to be the most successful person to emerge from *America's Got Talent*.

But that doesn't mean he's relaxed his work ethic. When asked what advice he would give others, Fator said, "Never stop working. Always work. When you stop working the dream dies. And if you love what you're doing, if you love to perform, it doesn't matter if you're in front of an elementary school group of 20 kids, or 20 million people on *America's Got Talent*."[10]

If working with a puppet takes thirty years of diligent practice, no wonder it takes so long for some of us to grow in our walk with Christ. So start now!

We don't arrive at immediate spiritual and moral perfection the moment we receive Christ as Savior. Yes, we're forgiven immediately. We're given the promise of eternal life immediately. We instantly become part of God's family. But growing to maturity—acquiring the divine nature, escaping the corruption of the world, and learning to withstand the pressures of life—all that takes time and requires diligence.

THE MOTIVATION FOR DILIGENCE

Second Peter 1:5 offers further motivation for adding diligence in our lives. It says, "For this very reason, giving all diligence, add to your faith."

Those words demand context. We're obviously breaking into the middle of a thought, so let's review the thought as it's presented in the prior verses. Verses 3 and 4 tell us we already have an endless reservoir of grace. In other words, the money is in the bank. The vault is full. The resources are stockpiled and allocated for us. Everything we need for a successful life and for a godly character has been provided.

Everything covers it all. Everything you need to overcome temptation, achieve maturity, and develop purpose and productivity. Everything you need to be a better husband, wife, father, mother, employee, employer, student, witness, example, influencer, and leader. Everything you need to have an exciting personal ministry that will never be in vain. All these divine resources are transmitted to you through God's very great and precious promises.

Understanding that truth lights a fuse of motivation that ignites our hearts and moves us toward diligence in our daily lives.

For more than a century, psychologists have tried to figure out why some people are more motivated than others. Frederick Winslow Taylor began studying this topic in the late 1800s and concluded the major factor in motivation was money. Years later, Elton Mayo found people were motivated by whether or not their bosses watched them work. A few years after that, Abraham Maslow connected motivation to our core needs. More recently, studies point to dopamine levels in the brain as a contributing factor.[11]

There may be many factors in a person's motivation levels, but I can give you one that overrides all others. When you understand what Jesus Christ has done for you, what He can do for you, what He offers you, the riches available to you, and the plans and expectations He has for you, you've found the greatest single motivation for diligent living the world will ever know.

Let me show you how important diligence was to Peter. He devoted nine verses in this passage (2 Peter 1:3–11) to the subject of living a godly life, and twice he exhorted his readers to be diligent. He was reminding Christians of our sacred obligation to maximize the resources God has given us.

- Verse 5 says, "But also for this very reason, giving all *diligence*, add to your faith."
- Verse 10 says, "Therefore, brethren, be even more *diligent* to make your call and election sure, for if you do these things you will never stumble."

God has given us everything we need through His very great and precious promises so we can live a truly godly life. *For this very reason*, we must diligently use the available resources and do our part. We must diligently acquire the special components of our faith Peter was about to identify for us. And we must be even more diligent to make our calling and election sure.

This is the very same message Paul employed to challenge and motivate the Philippians to an active pursuit of holiness in their lives:

"Therefore, my beloved, as you have always obeyed, not as in my presence only, but now much more in my absence, work out your own salvation with fear and trembling; for it is God who works in you both to will and to do for His good pleasure" (Phil. 3:12–13).

Peter and Paul had the same philosophy: God has given us everything we need, but that's no excuse for being lazy and passive in the Christian experience. We're to take what God has produced in us and work it out in our everyday lives. We're to take the promises God has given us and diligently apply them. And this is serious business. We're to do it with fear and trembling.

After professional driver Will Power—yes, that's his name, William Steven Power, but he appropriately goes by Will Power—won the Indianapolis 500, he told a reporter, "I'm really enjoying my racing. I've never been so motivated. I'm fitter than I've ever been, mentally on the game. I think once you get to this part of your career, you realize that you're not going to be doing this forever. So you've got to enjoy it and you've got to go for it when you've got it, because, you know, probably only another five years at maximum, and you're retired."[12]

Why don't you take those words and paraphrase them like this: "I'm really enjoying my Christian race. I've never been so motivated. I'm fitter than I've ever been in godliness and goodness, and I'm excited to know I'll be doing this forever. I'm going to enjoy it and go for it, because forever and ever I'll be loving God and living for Him. I'm going to do it passionately from the start, diligently. With His help, I'm determined to be full of godly willpower."

THE METHOD OF DILIGENCE

Now let's look at a small word in verse 5, but one that had a large influence on Peter's message—the term *add*. While this word is only printed once in the text of 2 Peter 1, it is assumed six additional times. Verses 5 through 7 say, in effect, "Giving all diligence, *add* to your faith virtue, *add* to virtue knowledge, *add* to knowledge self-control, *add* to self-control perseverance, *add* to perseverance godliness, *add* to godliness brotherly kindness, and *add* to brotherly kindness love."

The word *add* is the translation of a Greek term that described "the leader of a chorus." In ancient plays, the choirmaster was responsible for supplying everything his group needed. William Barclay explained it like this:

> All these plays needed large choruses and were, therefore, very expensive to produce. In the great days of Athens there were public-spirited citizens who voluntarily took on the duty, at their own expense, of collecting, maintaining, training and equipping such choruses. . . . The men who undertook these duties out of their own pocket and out of love for their city were called *choregoi*. . . . The word has a certain lavishness in it. It never means to equip in any . . . miserly way; it means lavishly to pour out everything that is necessary for a noble performance.[13]

Just think of it like this: we are to express the same diligence toward godliness that the ancients exhibited toward their productions and plays; the same diligence toward godliness that Olympic athletes demonstrated as they prepared for their Olympic events; the same diligence toward godliness that was resident in Peter and Paul and the majority of the other disciples of Jesus Christ.

That, it seems to me, is the heart of diligence—its meaning, its motivation, and its method.

UNDERTAKING THE HABITS OF DILIGENCE

In my own experience I've learned it's not enough to have a heart of diligence; we must translate that heart into habits.

Many years ago in my first tour of duty as a pastor, the Lord gave me two verses of Scripture that I adopted as my life verses, and they have been like a slogan across my heart ever since. These verses don't include the term *diligence*, but they define it perfectly. You find them in Colossians 3:23–24: "And whatever you do, do it heartily, as to the Lord and not to men, knowing that from the Lord you will receive the reward of the inheritance; for you serve the Lord Christ."

When the Lord impressed me with those verses, I asked Him to help me live according to them and to make them the formula for His work through me. I want you to know I've fallen short of that standard many times. Even so, I never lose sight of this goal: to live for the Lord with nothing held back, full throttle; to do whatever He asks me to do with all my heart, never looking back with regret, fully engaged in His purpose for my life.

If the heart of diligence is found in 2 Peter 1, I believe the habits of diligence are found here in Colossians 3. After years of repeating these verses to myself and others, thinking about them, and trying to live by them, let me share the four habits I try to practice every day.

LOOK AROUND: "WHATEVER YOU DO"

I call the first habit "look around" because diligence is a lifestyle. Colossians 3:23 begins with the words *whatever you do*. That covers a vast territory of activity. It means that nothing falls outside of this instruction to the believer. It's not just about spiritual habits or religious routines. It's not just about your life at church. These words cover everything.

If you read the entire third chapter of Colossians, you'll see that verses 23 and 24 are set in the context of everyday life. They come at the end of a section that deals with husbands, wives, children, fathers, and bond servants.

These verses implore us to dive into all our tasks diligently. This includes everything from fixing a leaky faucet, changing diapers, and paying bills to resolving conflicts between loved ones, finding a job, making our marriages stronger—you name it. The word *whatever* means whatever. It covers anything and everything we do as followers of Christ no matter who we are.

Sometimes the need for diligence is thrust upon us without any warning. Such was my experience in the final months of 2013. For more than three years we prayed, researched, and wrote in preparation for the publication of *The Jeremiah Study Bible*, which was to be released in November of that year. The marketing department at our media ministry planned a special Thanksgiving promotion to introduce this new resource to as many people as possible. Here was their plan: "If you order a *Jeremiah Study Bible* over the Thanksgiving holiday week-end, Dr. Jeremiah will sign your Bible, and you will have it in time for Christmas."

I was told we anticipated a couple thousand copies would be ordered, and although that would be challenging, I'd done similar things before. But almost immediately we knew we were in trouble. We were over-whelmed with orders. We had more than two thousand orders in the first half of the first day of the campaign.

I will never forget the despair I felt when I began to realize what was ahead of me in the first two weeks of December. Every day when I showed up at my office, there would be a train of carts waiting out-side my office door, each cart loaded down with more than one hundred Bibles. I did not know how I would do it, but I was determined not to disappoint anyone who had believed in this study Bible. Each morning I started signing Bibles at eight o'clock, and I signed them until late in the afternoon. Two people helped me: one opened the Bible to the right page; the other took the signed Bible and replaced it on the cart. We even pulled a couple of after-dinner shifts.

I remember thinking I could only sign one Bible at a time, and only receive one cart of Bibles at a time, and I would just concentrate on what each day brought. I lived on prayer, bananas, Gatorade, and the SiriusXM music channel. And amazingly, we finished on time! I've been told we set a new record for Bible signing—18,166 Bibles in two weeks—and everyone got their Bible by Christmas.

Each day as I viewed the task before me, I fought discouragement. But I focused on the joy this would bring the people who received these autographed Bibles and the joy of my heavenly Father as His Word was circulated to so many people. It was one day, one hour, one cart, one Bible, one signature, one moment at a time, with diligence.

As Martin Luther King Jr. put it:

> If it falls your lot to sweep streets in life, sweep streets like Michelangelo painted pictures. Sweep streets like Beethoven composed music. Sweep streets like Shakespeare wrote poetry. Sweep streets so well that all the hosts of heaven and earth will have to pause and say, "Here lived a great street sweeper, who swept his job well."[14]

LOOK WITHIN: "DO IT HEARTILY"

That leads to the next habit: looking within and recognizing that diligence is strenuous. Paul used the word *heartily*, which literally means "from the soul," or "from the innermost fabric of one's being."

In the New Testament there are three possible heart temperatures. First, there is the cold heart. Matthew 24:12 describes the people of the last days as those whose love for God shall wax cold.

Then in Revelation 3 we read of those whose hearts are lukewarm. Writing to the church in Laodicea, the Lord described His disdain for a half-lived life: "I know your works, that you are neither cold nor hot. I could wish you were cold or hot. So then, because you are lukewarm, and neither cold nor hot, I will vomit you out of My mouth" (vv. 15–16).

Finally, there is the burning heart. Luke 24:32 tells of two disciples who talked with Jesus on the road to Emmaus and described their experience like this: "Did not our heart burn within us while He talked with us on the road, and while He opened the Scriptures to us?"

A cold heart, a lukewarm heart, and a burning-hot heart. Which one are you?

One of the most motivating books I've read in recent years is called *Grit*. The author, Angela Duckworth, defined grit as a "combination of passion and perseverance that [makes] high achievers special."[15]

The powerful stories in this book chronicle what people are willing to sacrifice to achieve their dreams. For example, Olympic swimmer Rowdy Gaines "tabulated how much practice it took to develop the stamina, technique, confidence, and judgment to win an Olympic gold medal. In the eight-year period leading up to the 1984 games, he swam, in increments of fifty-yard laps, at least twenty thousand miles. Of course, if you add in the years before and after, the odometer goes even higher."

Gaines said, "I swam around the world for a race that lasted forty-nine seconds."[16]

Let me pose a question for all of us who are followers of Christ: If diligence would drive a man to swim around the world to prepare for a forty-nine-second race, what kind of diligence should we be striving for with eternity as our goal?

I think I hear the apostle Paul saying, "They do it to obtain a perishable crown, but we for an imperishable crown" (1 Cor. 9:25).

Diligence is strenuous. It means we serve the Lord and strive for eternity with all our hearts.

LOOK ABOVE: "AS TO THE LORD"

The real secret to developing diligence in your life is found in the next phrase of Colossians 3:23. We look above and live this way "as to the Lord and not to men." This was a recurring theme in Paul's letters. He wrote:

- "For none of us lives to himself, and no one dies to himself. For if we live, we live to the Lord; and if we die, we die to the Lord. Therefore, whether we live or die, we are the Lord's" (Rom. 14:7–8).
- "And whatever you do in word or deed, do all in the name of the Lord Jesus, giving thanks to God the Father through Him" (Col. 3:17).

We must put our best efforts into all we do because, ultimately, we're not working for a human employer to earn money or for a human corporation to make profits, or even for ourselves to build success. We are serving Christ in order to please Him.

In his book *Lyrics*, songwriter and producer Oscar Hammerstein II told of seeing a picture of the Statue of Liberty taken from a helicopter. The photo showed the top of the statue's head, and Hammerstein was impressed with the detail and excellence the sculptor had taken to complete a portion of the statue that few eyes would ever see. "He was artist enough," wrote Hammerstein, "to finish off this part of the statue with as much care as he had devoted to her face and her arms and the torch and everything that people can see as they sail up the bay."[17]

Michelangelo, painting in some obscure corner of the Sistine Chapel, was asked by one of his helpers why he lavished such attention on a part of the ceiling no one would ever see. He replied, "God will see."[18]

One way you can practice the habit of working diligently for the Lord is to simply pause throughout the day and look up. Remind yourself that God sees everything and that you are living to please Him. Then return to whatever you were doing and give it your all, knowing God smiles when He sees you working to honor Him.

LOOK AHEAD: "YOU WILL RECEIVE THE REWARD"

That brings us to the best part: looking ahead. The same God who has given you everything you need for a life of godliness will also reward you for living that way. My life verses end by saying, "Knowing that from the Lord you will receive the reward of the inheritance; for you serve the Lord Christ" (Col. 3:24).

This is the same reward Peter mentioned as he wrapped up his paragraph in 2 Peter 1. Peter commanded believers to add one quality after another to their faith so that "an entrance will be supplied . . . abundantly into the everlasting kingdom of our Lord and Savior Jesus Christ" (v. 11).

When Elvis Presley was in his heyday, he hired a bodyguard named Sonny West, who served him with all the energy he could muster. Sonny broke into the king's inner circle and became part of what was known as the Memphis Mafia. Elvis was the best man at Sonny's wedding, and the two were close friends. Sonny even appeared in a movie with Presley.

But after Elvis died, Sonny's life began to spiral downward. He and his wife both battled cancer and faced foreclosure because of mounting medical bills. He eventually began selling all his Elvis Presley memorabilia, including the jewelry Presley gave him. "I don't want to leave my family behind, penniless, leave them with nothing," he said. "I just feel very depressed."

Inside Edition, which reported the story months before his death in 2017, said, "Sonny West once rode Elvis Presley's coattails to fame as his best friend and bodyguard, but decades later, the glitz and glamor has faded away."[19]

That story provides us with a startling contrast. Here was a man who served the "king" with all his heart, but the experience ended, the glitz evaporated, and the glory faded.

I, however, have a King I'm serving with all my heart, and the best for me is yet to come. All of us who live full throttle for Jesus Christ—all of us who diligently advance from glory to glory, all of us who do whatever we do heartily as unto the Lord—will receive our reward of an eternal inheritance with Him.

There will be no end to the hallelujahs! No end to the joy! No end to the fellowship with our Savior and His people! No end to the days of our lives or the answers to our prayers! No end to our passion and purpose, for even in heaven His servants will serve Him.

THE MOST IMPORTANT THING IN THE WORLD

Let me conclude this chapter with what Charles Spurgeon said:

> If I have any message to give from my own bed of sickness, it would be this—if you do not wish to be full of regrets when you are obliged to lie still, work while you can. If you desire to make a sick bed as soft as it can be, do not stuff it with the mournful reflection that you wasted time while you were in health and strength. People said to me years ago, "You will break your constitution down with preaching ten times a week," and the like. Well, if I have done so, I am glad of it. I would do the same again. If I had fifty constitutions I would rejoice to break them down in the service of the Lord Jesus Christ. You young men that are strong, overcome the wicked one and fight for the Lord while you can. You will never regret having done all that lies in you for our blessed Lord and Master. Crowd as much as you can into every day, and postpone no work till tomorrow. "Whatsoever thy hand findeth to do, do it with thy might."[20]

Lavishly follow Christ with all that you are and all that you have. No sacrifice can be considered too expensive nor any requirement too demanding.

When Jesus was asked by a lawyer to identify the most important of all the commandments, He answered, "'You shall love the LORD your God with all your heart, with all your soul, and with all your mind.' This is the first and great commandment" (Matt. 22:37–38).

This is the most important thing in the world. Nothing else is even close! So I urge you to serve the King with all your heart, and make sure you're serving the right King. Serve Him by diligently adding one virtue to another in your spiritual résumé. Develop a muscular faith!

And here's the best part: you can begin right now, wherever you are, with whatever you're doing—as long as you're doing it for the Lord. Do the next thing that comes your way, and do it diligently for the Lord. Do whatever you would normally do when you lay down this book, but do it differently now. Do it consciously for Him.

Does your floor need mopping? Does your child need help with homework? Do you need to make a business appointment, rehearse a song for the church choir, or prepare for a class?

All right, good! Do it with enthusiasm, with diligence, and do it for Christ!

Start right now. Whatever you do next, do it with all your heart. Whether you eat or drink or whatever you do, do it for Him who has given you all you need for life and godliness through His great and precious promises.

Do it for Jesus.

Whether you eat or drink, or whatever
you do, do all to the glory of God.
—1 CORINTHIANS 10:31

Chapter 3

MORAL EXCELLENCE

After Tim Nybo graduated from college in 2010, he decided to start a business in China. He packed up his few belongings, bought a one-way ticket, and moved to a Chinese manufacturing city, although he couldn't speak the language or even use chopsticks.

At the time the United States' economy was in recession, but the Chinese economy was thriving. Nybo had five thousand dollars in his pocket, but that didn't take him far. He started teaching English classes to cover his living expenses. And all the time he was mulling over ideas for a product he could export and sell.

An idea came to him when the market for iPads and tablets boomed. He partnered with a manufacturing company to produce cases for the devices. He poured enormous effort into the business, but he forgot one thing: quality control. As a result, he ordered thousands of cases for electronic tablets that were defective. They didn't fit the tablets they were supposed to match, and the buttons were in the wrong places. Not surprisingly, the young businessman lost his shirt.[1]

But Tim Nybo learned a lesson that shaped his subsequent career as an entrepreneur in San Diego. "We wanted a product built to our exact specifications, but we neglected quality control from the beginning. . . . Our experience taught us that people who involve themselves in the quality control process receive substantially better products."

Nybo's greatest takeaway from the experience: "Product quality, not profit margins, is the key to long-term success."[2] As a result of this principle, he's become so successful that others now learn from his lessons and leadership.

Quality control will make or break any commercial enterprise. Quality control is essential in business, in public utilities, in agriculture, in education, in sports—in every area of life. And it is vital to our personalities too. You and I are not exempt from the need for personal quality control. If we're going to be strong and effective people who can withstand the pressures of this world and bear a testimony and leave behind a legacy, we must be people of quality.

The Bible has a word for that: *virtue*.

That's a word we seldom hear anymore, but it's in the Bible. It's the Bible's quality-control division, and the apostle Peter told us we should be diligent about adding virtue to our faith (2 Peter 1:5).

WHAT IS VIRTUE?

Notice the word *virtue* occurs twice in 2 Peter 1:3–5. In verse 3, we're told God has "called us by glory and *virtue*," and in verse 5 we are to give all diligence to add to our "faith *virtue*." In other words, we are called *by* virtue, and we are called *to* virtue.

Virtue speaks to the quality of our character, to spiritual excellence and moral goodness. A person of virtue is a quality person—a person of integrity, kindness, goodness, generosity, graciousness; someone who is, or genuinely tries to be, above reproach.

True virtue is born of faith. Notice how Peter put it in 2 Peter 1:5: "But also for this very reason, giving all diligence, add to your faith virtue."

Virtue has its beginning in trusting God, in placing your full weight on the worthiness of God's Word. If this sounds challenging, you're probably overthinking it. For so many Christ-followers this is one of the simplest and most wondrous steps we take in our faith journey. We simply and fully trust in the Lord to save us from our sins—and from there we begin cultivating Christlikeness in our lives.

In June 2017, *Christianity Today* had a story about a young man named Abbas Hameed who grew up in Iraq. One of eight children, Abbas was raised with little spiritual background, but when his father came to Christ, Abbas was amazed at the change in the man's personality.

At age nineteen, Abbas completed training for the Iraqi police academy. Not long after, in March 2003, American soldiers entered his area. He decided to go to Tikrit and join the United States military police, where he became part of a SWAT squad.

One spring day in 2005 Abbas was directing traffic when a suspicious vehicle came toward him. He motioned for the car to stop, but it kept coming. He was preparing to shoot at the driver when the car, now only about fifteen feet away, detonated. Abbas was thrown into the air and hurled to the ground. Stunned but not seriously injured, he decided God had saved his life.

Two years passed, and Abbas was assigned to the army's Eighty-Second Airborne Division, where he met Sergeant Scott Young. "I realized there was something different about him," Abbas said. "He had a book in his knee pocket all the time. Every time we had a break, I observed him reading, and I was intrigued. Scott told me it was the Bible, and I started to read it every day for myself. I kept going back to Scott to ask questions about what I was reading."

Because of Sergeant Young's witness, Abbas placed his faith in Jesus Christ. He later wrote, "The next morning, the whole military company noticed a change, just as I had noticed the change in my father after his own conversion. I had a smile on my face, and I wasn't as mean as before. God had worked a huge and powerful transformation."[3]

See how this works? When you place your faith in Christ for salvation, He begins transforming you so you can accept His gifts of everything you need for a godly life. By His grace, you grow, change, and can diligently add virtue to your faith. Whatever outward manifestation of "meanness" you formerly expressed—impatience, gossip, defensiveness, harsh words—can be replaced by virtue through God's love.

Faith creates virtue and also sustains it. Trusting God with your problems and your worries about the future is one of the simplest ways to practice virtue daily. That trust sustains excellence and quality living.

In her book *Let's Be Friends*, Elizabeth Hoagland wrote about her friend Cassie Soete, whose husband, George, told her on their twentieth wedding anniversary that he was leaving her to marry someone else. Cassie and George had six children, ages two to nineteen. Over the next four years, George made eight appearances in their lives. But Cassie prayed nonstop for him, even though her heart was broken.

"I hit the wall after the four-year mark," she said. "Anger took over, and I had a little chat with God. I told Him He would have to be the one to fix our marriage, that I was done trying. That was the beginning of the total strength I found in my awesome God. My faith became immovable with every step I took, with every breath I breathed."

George began to see the changes in Cassie's life. One night, unable to sleep in his apartment, he opened the Bible Cassie and the kids had given him for Christmas. George was so overwhelmed that he gave his life to Christ.

"Our faithful, awesome God restored our broken marriage to the fullest," Cassie said. "God showed His power by reuniting two broken souls to help others heal their marriage."

George passed away in 2015, but Cassie said, "I see after one year of being alone that God continues to be my awesome God. He lifts me up even now as I write these very difficult words. He has never left my side. He's the hope I cling to."[4]

That's how faith sustains virtue. When you hit a wall or encounter a problem, take it to the Lord. Cast your burden on Him. He gives you a promise—one of those great and precious promises we studied in 2 Peter 1:4—that strengthens your moral fiber. It undergirds your hope and positive spirit. It energizes your testimony and makes you a person of excellence. That is virtue.

THE MORAL QUALITY OF CHRIST: HE AIMED TO PLEASE GOD

Disneyland and Disney World—the whole world of Disney—have been built on quality control. That principle began with Walt Disney, who inspired deep loyalty in his employees. One of his associates, Stormy Palmer, said, "Walt's inspiration and enthusiasm made over-achievers of all of us at the studio. You wanted to please him. Walt was more than a boss. He was like a father to me."[5]

People work diligently to produce quality work because they want to please someone above them. It's the same with a quality life—we want to please Someone above us. And that's the secret of virtue—the quality-control division of morality and character. In its essence, it's a desire to please our heavenly Father.

In John 8, our Lord was having a discussion with His critics, the Pharisees, who resented the quality of His life because His moral excellence was visibly superior to theirs. And so He told them His secret. He said in verses 28 and 29: "When you lift up the Son of Man, then you will know that I am He, and that I do nothing of Myself; but as My Father taught Me, I speak these things. And He who sent me is with Me. The Father has not left Me alone, for I always do those things that *please* Him." The secret to Jesus' virtue was His singular focus on pleasing His Father.

Likewise, in John 5:30, Jesus said, "I seek not to *please* myself but him who sent me" (NIV).

Now, here is the fascinating thing. On two different occasions at different phases of Jesus' earthly life, God the Father spoke audibly from heaven with the same essential message: He was pleased with Jesus Christ and the life He was living on earth.

AT HIS BAPTISM

The first time God audibly expressed His pleasure with Jesus was in Matthew 3, when Jesus was baptized. When our Lord came up out of the water, the heavens opened, and the Holy Spirit descended like a dove and rested on Him, "and suddenly a voice came from heaven, saying, 'This is My beloved Son, in whom *I am well pleased*'" (v. 17).

God the Father knew Jesus' life from His birth until that point. He had watched as Jesus was laid in the manger. He saw Jesus grow through childhood until age twelve, when the boy Jesus tarried in Jerusalem wanting to be about His Father's business. His omniscient eyes took in every day of our Lord's teenage years as He grew in wisdom and stature and in favor with God and man. He watched the Lord enter the field of carpentry, building houses and buildings, and He saw Him lay aside His hammer and trowel to enter the ministry. Now, as Jesus began His official work at His baptism, the entire Trinity merged together to affirm the moral quality and virtue of Jesus.

God the Son in the waters of baptism; God the Spirit from the parted heavens; and God the Father pronouncing the truth about the excellence of a well-lived thirty years, saying, "This is My beloved Son, in whom I am well pleased."

Let me pause here to say something to the dads and moms and grandparents reading this: the heavenly Father is giving us an example to follow. I don't want to use the word *pride* here to characterize God, but in human terms you can almost sense a tone of, well, satisfaction and pleasure in God's voice. *This is My beloved Son. I am so pleased with Him.*

Our own children need to hear similar words from us. A child's self-image is largely based on their perception of what their parents think of them. I know we can overdo it and brag on our children too much, but most of us err in the other direction. We don't give our children the affirmation they need.

Recently my first grandson graduated from college. He did it in three years and with honors. I left the church where I pastor in the care of others for that weekend because I wanted to be there for him at the ceremony. I wanted to look him in the eye and tell him how proud I am of him.

Wess Stafford, who for many years was president of Compassion International, wrote, "I happen to believe that children carry with them at all times a little invisible chalkboard, a blank slate that they hold up to us saying essentially, 'Please tell me something. Something about myself. Something about my life, my world.' . . . Sometimes we miss their silent pleas for affirmation."[6]

Incidentally, the reverse is also true. We don't often mention it, but parents need to know that our children are proud of us too. In 2019, Tiger Woods won the Masters Tournament after years of failed attempts, not to mention scandals and humiliations. As soon as the tournament was over, a reporter asked what his children said to him when he won. Tiger said he couldn't hear them because everyone was screaming, but he added, "I think—well, I hope, I hope they are proud of me. I hope they are proud of their dad."[7]

When was the last time you expressed your appreciation and esteem for those nearest you? "I'm so pleased you're my wife." "I'm so proud you're my mom." "Son, I'm proud of you." What power in these words!

When the heavenly Father affirmed Jesus and told others how pleased He was with Him, He also showed us how to affirm our own children and loved ones. We're to let the world know we're proud of those we love. Nothing builds a person's confidence more than that.

AT HIS TRANSFIGURATION

The second time almighty God spoke audibly from heaven into Christ's ministry was at the Transfiguration, arguably the most unusual episode in the life of Jesus. To understand it, we have to remember who Christ was—He was fully God in every way, divine, eternal, the Ancient of Days, who had set aside His glory for a brief season, entered into humanity through a virgin's womb, and became a man while remaining God. During His earthly life, His divine glory was veiled from sight. But on this one occasion Christ allowed His inner circle to get a glimpse of His true glory.

Matthew 17 says, "He was transfigured before them. His face shone like the sun, and His clothes became as white as the light. . . . Behold, a bright cloud overshadowed them; and suddenly a voice came out of the cloud, saying, 'This is My beloved Son, in whom *I am well pleased*. Hear Him!'" (vv. 2, 5).

The voice was such a clap of thunderous power that the disciples fell on the ground, facedown and terrified. But Jesus came and touched them and told them not to be afraid. Here, in the middle of His ministry, God again affirmed that He was pleased with the way Jesus was conducting Himself, with His excellence of speech and character, and with the holy and righteous quality of His life. The disciples were called to listen to

Him, believing and obeying His words. How this must have strengthened Jesus Christ for His coming work at Calvary.

Peter never forgot that moment, and he brought it up here in this chapter—in 2 Peter 1:17—when he wrote, "For He received from God the Father honor and glory when such a voice came to Him from the Excellent Glory: 'This is My beloved Son, in whom I am well pleased.'"

What if God the Father spoke from heaven right now in a clap of thunder with words so distinct that we were jolted to the floor in terror? Can you imagine that? His message would be the same. He is pleased with His Son. He is pleased with Christ, and we must believe and obey all the words of our Savior.

God the Father was pleased with the One who sought in all things to always do that which pleased God. And that is what you and I are also called to do. That is virtue, the sterling excellence of a life well-lived.

THE MORAL QUALITY OF CHRIST-FOLLOWERS: WE AIM TO PLEASE GOD

Let's take this a step further. Just as Christ was pleasing to God, the Bible teaches that Christ-followers are to "make it our goal to please him" (2 Cor. 5:9 NIV). And how do we please God? By living a virtuous life, a life of moral quality.

That might sound intimidating, even overwhelming. But it's not. Pastor Kevin DeYoung explains,

> When we hear the language of "pleasing God," some of us panic because we only relate to God as a judge. But he is also our Father. If you think, *I have to please God with my obedience because he is my judge*, you will undermine the good news of justification by faith alone. But you ought

to reason this way: "I've been acquitted. The Lord is my righteousness. I am justified fully and adopted into the family of God for all eternity. I am so eager to please my Father and live for him."[8]

When we know God as a loving and forgiving Father, the quest for virtue becomes a joy and an adventure. Yes, we work hard to develop virtue and please Him. But we don't do this from a desire to gain His love and acceptance. Instead, because He already loves and accepts us, we strive to please Him with a life well-lived.

And this isn't a vague proposition. The Bible gives us specific instructions. I can't include in these pages every biblical reference related to pleasing God, but I can give you three ways to practice this kind of virtue based on Paul's first letter to the Thessalonians.

LIVE ABOVE THE FRAY

First Thessalonians 4:1–2 says, "We urge and exhort in the Lord Jesus that you should abound more and more, just as you received from us how you ought to walk and to please God; for you know what commandments we gave you through the Lord Jesus."

These words are written to you just as much as they were addressed to the original audience of Christians in Thessalonica. So how then should you live? The next verses provide an answer: "God's will is for you to be holy, so stay away from all sexual sin. Then each of you will control his own body and live in holiness and honor" (vv. 3–4 NLT).

You can't talk about the biblical quality of virtue without dealing with moral and sexual purity. When you diligently add virtue to your faith, that includes incorporating God's model for your sexual conduct.

In Paul's day, as in our day, there was a lot of premarital and extramarital sex. But from the beginning of creation, from the days of Adam and Eve, such behavior does not represent God's will or His plan for you. He created the intimacy of sex to be something exclusively enjoyed within the union of a covenant marriage between one man and one woman (Gen. 2:23–25; Matt. 19:4–6). It pleases God when you reject the world's immorality and practice virtue in your life. That is moral excellence. That is purity. That is virtue. And it is rare today.

In his book about personal purity, Randy Alcorn wrote of a man named Eric who came to see him one day. Eric flopped down into a chair and said, "I'm really mad at God." Randy was surprised because he knew Eric grew up in a Christian home and married a Christian girl. He asked Eric why he was mad at God.

"Because last week I committed adultery."

Randy absorbed that, then asked, "I can see why God would be mad at you. But why are *you* mad at *God*?"

Eric answered that for several months he'd battled a strong mutual attraction with a woman at work, and he prayed that God would keep him from immorality. But Eric gave in. Now he was furious with God for letting him yield to temptation.

Randy asked Eric if he'd asked his wife to pray for him during this time of temptation and if he'd taken definite steps to avoid this woman.

"Well . . . no," said Eric. "We went out for lunch almost every day."

There was a big book lying on the desk, and Randy took his hand and started pushing it across the surface as Eric watched. The book came closer and closer to the edge. Randy prayed aloud, "O Lord, please keep this book from falling!" But he kept pushing the book, and God did not suspend the laws of gravity. The book fell to the floor with a loud *thump*. Randy looked at Eric and said, "I'm mad at God. I asked Him to keep my book from falling . . . but He let me down!"

Randy wrote, "Every day, Christian men and women forfeit future happiness for the sake of temporary sexual stimulation. With every little glance that fuels our lust, we push ourselves closer to the edge, where gravity will take over and bring our lives crashing down."[9]

How can you stay away from sexual sin? Let me give you five ways to protect your virtue.

Fill Your Heart with Jesus

First, make it the greatest ambition of your life to please God. If you're inflamed with that motivation, it's much harder to fall into sin. To overcome sin and temptation, fill your heart with Jesus. God made you; He loves you; He sent Christ to die for you; He wants a daily relationship with you; He wants to bless you; He has a purpose for your life; He has an eternal home for you. Why would you not want to please Him more than anything in the world? Believe me, that motivation is your greatest path to holiness.

Fill Your Mind with Scripture

Second, fill your mind with Scripture. This is the principle of displacement. In science, this is called the Archimedes' principle. According to historical tradition, an ancient king asked the famous Greek scientist and inventor Archimedes to determine if the local goldsmith had deceitfully included materials other than gold in the royal crown. Archimedes couldn't figure out how to reach a conclusion.

One day, while taking a bath, he submerged himself in the tub, and water overflowed onto the floor. Archimedes realized that any object immersed in a fluid is acted upon by an upward force equal to the weight of the fluid displaced by the object. In other words, the principle of displacement. That gave him the formula for resolving the question about the crown, as the weight of pure gold would be heavier than any impurities.

In spiritual terms, this means that when you take the Bible and submerge it into your brain, it has a way of displacing other thoughts, and this pleases God. One way of accomplishing this "submersion" is by meditating on passages such as 1 Thessalonians 4: "God's will is for you to be holy, so stay away from all sexual sin. Then each of you will control his own body and live in holiness and honor" (vv. 3–4 NLT).

Fill Your Routines with Rules

Third, create rules for yourself that you simply won't violate. People don't like rules anymore. They say, "Oh, I don't want to be legalistic." But without rules, no classroom could operate, no city streets would be safe, no bank could be trusted, and no government could function. If everything and everyone else in the world needs some rules, don't you think you might need some too?

Early in his ministry, after seeing a number of prominent evangelists fall into sin, Dr. Billy Graham decided he would never be alone with a woman who wasn't his wife. This decision became known as "The Billy Graham Rule." He was not only protecting himself against temptation; he was also protecting himself against the possibility of untrue perceptions or slanderous accusations.

While the Billy Graham Rule isn't a command from the Lord, it's a habit I've practiced all of my ministerial life as one way to honor and love my wife.

As disciples of Jesus seeking virtue, we must be people who build fences, set rules, establish boundaries, and establish lifestyles that keep us from undue temptation. Therefore, have some rules for yourself about platonic friendships, Internet use, your standards and practices in dating, what you do when you're traveling alone on business, and so on. Think through these issues and establish guardrails for your life.

Fill Your Friendships with Accountability

During the 1960s, the term *accountability partner* was coined by a diet program as a buddy system to help you lose weight. In the 1990s, Christians used the term to describe people who helped each other with moral purity. A study by the University of Scranton found that not having an accountability partner is one reason 92 percent of people do not accomplish their New Year's resolutions.[10]

Our passage in 2 Peter says that God has given you everything you need for life and godliness, and this includes other people. It can be a great help to have someone with whom you can be honest and accountable, so ask God to show you that person. He can lead you to someone who will provide an extra layer of protection in your life.

If you have a close friend you trust, make a pact with that friend to hold each other accountable to live in holiness.

Fill Your Soul with Resolve

Finally, let me leave you with a general suggestion: do whatever it takes to guard yourself against temptation. The magnetic lure of temptation is hitting all of us, including our children, harder than any other time in history, largely because of the combination of sexual freedom and electronic access.

As a young man, Daniel "purposed in his heart that he would not defile himself" (Dan. 1:8). Joseph ran from Potiphar's wife even as she was trying to snatch the clothes off him (Gen. 39:12).

Jesus said about sexual sin, "If your right eye causes you to sin, pluck it out and cast it from you. . . . And if your right hand causes you to sin, cut it off and cast it from you" (Matt. 5:29–30). He wasn't speaking literally, of course. He was using extreme language to make a point: do whatever it takes to withstand moral temptation.

If it takes counseling, get it. If it takes giving up your electronics, give them up. If it takes being part of a support group, join it. Do whatever it takes! Don't wait another day! Do it now before the book falls off the table!

LOVE YOUR FAITH FAMILY

You please God by living above the fray. But that's not all. The apostle Paul continued his explanation about pleasing God in 1 Thessalonians 4 by stressing the importance of loving others: "You ought to walk and to please God. . . . But concerning brotherly love you have no need that I should write to you, for you yourselves are taught by God to love one another; and indeed you do so toward all the brethren who are in all Macedonia" (vv. 1, 9–10).

The city of Thessalonica was in Macedonia near northern Greece. Paul traveled through that area starting churches—including in the cities of Philippi and Berea and other towns and villages. The believers in these new churches had never met each other. They came from different backgrounds and lived in different cities; some were wealthy, and some were poor. But when they became believers in Christ, instantly they had a common bond. Immediately they became brothers and sisters in Christ. They shared the deepest decision of their lives, and when they met, there was instant love between them.

Johnny Hunt described a demonstration he saw when he was attending middle school. The teacher dumped on the table all different types, sizes, and shapes of metal shavings—iron, steel, aluminum, and so forth. Then the teacher hauled out a powerful magnet and passed it over the metal. All the metals that were magnetic flew up to the magnet and were brought together and held together by an irresistible force. The metals that were not magnetically charged stayed on the table.

"Something similar happens spiritually," wrote Hunt. "When God puts His Spirit inside of us at the point of salvation, we are magnetized. As a result, all kinds of different people are brought together by the magnetic power of the Spirit of God."[11]

In the last several decades, the gospel has spread to many tribal areas of Papua New Guinea, and there's a song that rings out from the new churches. The words say, "You don't know me, I don't know you, but Jesus brings us together."[12]

Of course, our love for others isn't limited to other believers. God loves the whole world, and so do we. But here in 1 Thessalonians 4, Paul was emphasizing the unique, common, magnetic love that instantly binds together followers of Christ. The moment before receiving Jesus as Savior, we may be total strangers; but the moment He comes into our lives, we're brothers and sisters. And when we love each other in that way, God is pleased, and virtue shines forth in our hearts.

LEAD A QUIET LIFE

The apostle Paul wasn't finished with his discussion of the virtue of pleasing God in 1 Thessalonians 4. He had a final point to make—one that's more gripping now, perhaps, than ever. He told us we please God when we lead a quiet life. "Aspire to lead a quiet life, to mind your own business, and to work with your own hands, as we commanded you, that you may walk properly toward those who are outside, and that you may lack nothing" (vv. 11–12).

The word *quiet* here means "restful." Paul wasn't talking about living a silent life, but a serene one. One scholar said, "Paul was telling the Thessalonians to be less frantic, not less exuberant."[13] In other words, when we find Christ as Savior, we learn to trust Him without overreacting to every situation in life. There's a quiet confidence that fills our hearts, and we go about our business—our daily habits, our daily schedule—working hard and providing a good example for nonbelievers. This pleases God.

THEY'RE WATCHING

Terry Brubaker was driving near Gloversville, New York, when she saw $20, $50, and $100 bills flying into her windshield like confetti. She pulled over and began collecting the money, which amounted to roughly $6,600.

Without even considering her options, Brubaker went straight to the

Fulton County Sheriff's Office to turn the money in, and arrived just as the owner of the cash, Kim Steenburg, was filing a report. Kim had lost her husband in a car crash. She'd saved the money so she could go on a cruise and scatter her husband's ashes at sea. But she'd accidently left the money in an envelope on top of her car.[14]

One simple act of honesty meant the world to another person. On a planet where virtue is in short supply, we're thrilled to hear of someone who possesses such integrity. Stories like Terry's inspire us. And they remind us that we, too, can live with and reflect back to our Lord the godly virtues He has given us.

In *100 Bible Verses That Made America*, Robert Morgan wrote about President William McKinley, a dedicated Christian. When McKinley became president, he maintained his Christian testimony. One Sunday a fierce political opponent attended McKinley's church to spy on him during worship, expecting to find some trace of hypocrisy or showmanship. The man later wrote,

> I watched the President. I watched his face while he sang; I gave close attention to his countenance and attitude during all the opening service, and his interest in the earnest words which were spoken before the sacrament of the Lord's Supper was administered. And after a while, when I saw William McKinley get up from his place and go and kneel down at the altar, humbly, with the rest, and reverently take the Communion, and then, when he arose, quietly wipe away the traces of emotion from his eyes, his whole countenance and attitude showing the deepest religious emotion, I confess to you that I felt a great change coming over myself, and I said to myself, "A country which has a man like that at the head of its affairs is not so badly off, after all."[15]

People are watching you all the time. They're watching you at church, on campus, in the gym, in restaurants, at the office, in the factory, at the store. Perhaps some are hoping to see you mess up, lose your temper, cheat, cuss, or cut corners. But truly, I believe most of them are longing to see an honest person. A virtuous person—a person they would like to emulate in their own lives. You can be that person.

So, giving all diligence, add to your faith virtue. Make it your purpose this week and start today.

> *We . . . do not cease to pray for you, and to ask that*
> *you be filled with the knowledge of His will in all*
> *wisdom and spiritual understanding; that you may*
> *walk worthy of the Lord, fully pleasing Him.*
> —Colossians 1:9–10

Chapter 4

MENTAL FOCUS

Bob Dwyer loved college life. He had his own apartment near Northeastern Illinois University, where he pursued a degree in interdisciplinary studies. In April 2019, he took his final exam in a conflict communication course and then walked across the stage for his diploma in May. Nothing special about that for your typical college graduate—except for one detail: Bob is ninety years young and a great-grandfather. He is now the oldest student to receive a bachelor's degree since Northeastern started keeping records.

In 2010, Bob's wife of fifty-six years, Peggy, passed away. The couple's nine children are all grown with families of their own. Bob's career in manufacturing gave him financial security, so he decided to pursue his college degree simply for the sake of learning. "Education is always a plus and we can never have too much of it," he said. "I thought I knew a lot of things and I found out there was a lot I didn't know."[1]

That's true for our knowledge of God too. We think we know a lot, and then God shows us how much more there is to learn.

As we continue our exploration of 2 Peter 1:3–11, it's important to remember this was Peter's final letter to his followers, for he was nearing his execution. Soon after he sent his last epistle he was crucified as a martyr for Christ during the reign of the evil Roman emperor Nero. So as you read his message, remember that every word of this short letter was written by a man who knew this was his final, lasting instruction and encouragement to those who received Christ under his ministry.

With that in mind, you can't miss Peter's emphasis on knowledge.

Peter began and ended his book by striking this note. In his opening greeting, Peter wrote, "Grace and peace be multiplied to you in the knowledge of God and of Jesus our Lord" (2 Peter 1:2). Three chapters later he came full circle and ended his letter saying, "Grow in the grace and knowledge of our Lord and Savior Jesus Christ" (3:18). Between those two verses are thirteen other references to knowledge.

Knowledge and all it implies was clearly on Peter's mind as he faced the end of his life. Even then, he wanted to add knowledge to his virtue, and he exhorted us to do the same.

The wonderful thing about Scripture is its perpetual and powerful relevance. Peter's letters aren't just first-century documents written to people now dead. They are God's timeless and personal Word for you and me. Behind Peter's pen was the Spirit's inspiration, and we do well to imagine the Lord Jesus Himself speaking these words to us: *Grace and peace be multiplied to you in the knowledge of God. Grow in the knowledge of Me!*

IT'S NOT ABOUT YOUR IQ

From the portion of 2 Peter that prompted me to write this book you've learned how God's divine power gives you what you need for a great life through the knowledge of Him who called you by His glory. In personal terms, this means His power is transmitted into your life by His living promises.

But you have a role to play in this process through your actions and choices. You've examined how, with diligence, you must add virtue to your faith. But here's your next great step—now you must add knowledge to your virtue (2 Peter 1:5).

If you want to have everything you need in life, diligently keep adding knowledge to your stockpile of personal qualities. Knowledge and more knowledge! Always grow in the knowledge of our Lord Jesus Christ. Someone said, "An investment in knowledge pays the best interest."[2] That reflects the truth of Proverbs 10:14: "Wise people store up knowledge."

But what does that mean? How do you store up knowledge? How do you add it to your virtue? Well, let me get one misconception out of the way: you don't have to be a genius to do this, or even extremely smart. You don't have to be William James Sidis, one of the most brilliant minds in history and perhaps one of the smartest men who ever lived.

Born in 1898, Sidis was quickly recognized as a child prodigy. He read the *New York Times* before his second birthday. By age six he knew English, Latin, French, German, Russian, Hebrew, Turkish, and Armenian. He even invented his own language! Sidis entered Harvard at age eleven and graduated *cum laude*.

After graduation, Sidis told reporters he wanted to live "a perfect life," which to him meant getting away from the limelight. Sidis was tired of feeling like an oddity. He went into hiding, using aliases and moving from city to city. He wrote books under various names; no one knows how many because he had so many pseudonyms. In some of his writings he postulated the existence of dark matter, entropy, and thermodynamics. At one point he obsessively collected streetcar transfer tickets—about which he wrote another book.

Sidis was so successful in maintaining his privacy that no one knew where he was until the *New Yorker* sent a reporter to track down the "Boy Wonder," and the media scrutiny started all over. Sidis sued the *New Yorker* and won the case, but died suddenly at age forty-six from a brain hemorrhage.[3]

Here was a man who exceeded most others in intellect, but I wonder if he understood what genuine knowledge really is.

When the Lord tells you to diligently add knowledge to your virtue and to earnestly grow in the knowledge of the Lord Jesus Christ, He isn't talking about educational degrees or IQ levels. He's telling you to enroll in God's classroom and do as Jesus said in Matthew 11:29: "Take My yoke upon you and learn from Me."

When Peter spoke of knowledge, he was telling you to follow in his own footsteps and be a disciple. That involves three steps. There's a personal step when you tell the Lord, "I want to know You. I will follow You and be Your disciple, Your learner." There's a thoughtful step when you say, "I want to know Your Word. I want to study You and let the Word of God dwell in me richly." And there's a behavioral step when you say, "I will obey You. I want to learn how to live and walk in Your ways."

I WILL FOLLOW YOU

True *knowledge* begins with a yearning to know the Lord Jesus and to follow Him with all your heart. In Jesus are hidden "all the treasures of wisdom and knowledge" (Col. 2:3). Jesus said, "I am the . . . truth" (John 14:6). He didn't just come to tell the truth. He Himself is the embodiment of truth. He *is* the truth. The gateway to knowledge involves the decision to follow and learn from Him.

In New Testament terms, this is *discipleship*, and it includes two important stages.

MOVE FROM THE SHORELINE TO THE SAVIOR

Many Christians think there were only twelve disciples during Jesus' public ministry—one of whom, Judas Iscariot, was a traitor. But the word *disciple* was actually a common term for the followers of Christ in the early church. It's used thirty times in the book of Acts to describe those who became Christians. The very word *Christian*, which means "one like Christ," was coined to designate those who were known more generically as disciples. Acts 11:26 says, "The *disciples* were first called *Christians* in Antioch."

In the New Testament, the words *disciple* and *Christian* were synonyms. Would it make a difference in your church, or in your life, if you went back to the original terminology? I think it would. The next time someone asks you, "Are you a Christian?" try saying, "Yes, I'm a disciple of the Lord Jesus Christ." What a wonderful declaration!

In the New Testament, the word *disciple* meant "learner." In the ancient world, certain rabbis, teachers, and philosophers invited people to follow after them, and these people became learners. They followed the teachers from place to place in order to get to know them and their way of thinking; that is, to absorb their knowledge. They were disciples—learners.

No one knew this better than Peter himself. He never forgot the day Jesus came through his town of Capernaum, a fishing village on the shoreline of the Sea of Galilee. When Jesus called him, Peter left the shoreline of Galilee to follow the Savior.

Matthew 4:18–20 gives us the story. As Jesus walked along the beach, He "saw two brothers, Simon called Peter, and Andrew his brother, casting a net into the sea; for they were fishermen. Then He said to them, 'Follow Me, and I will make you fishers of men.' They immediately left their nets and followed Him."

They followed Him, all right. They followed Him through the streets of old Capernaum as He healed the sick and preached the kingdom.

They followed Him up the hillsides as He taught the multitudes and fed the crowds. They followed Him into fishing boats tossed in the storms, into homes packed with sinners, and into synagogues crammed with the curious. They watched Him turn water to wine, open the eyes of the blind, and battle with and cast out demons. They followed Him up and down the hot hills of Judea and into the angry streets of Jerusalem. They saw Him raise the dead, and they heard Him say, "I am the resurrection and the life" (John 11:25).

They listened to His sermons, and then they asked questions and grew in the knowledge of His teachings. Through it all, they came to know Him and to love Him. They grew confident of His love, power, authority, and righteousness.

With every passing day, they saw our Lord more clearly and loved Him more dearly; slowly they began to learn who He was and what He came to do. In time, they discerned what He wanted them to do. Their knowledge of Him wasn't simply academic; it was as personal as the deepest friendship in the world.

Let me say this to you: we all have to move from the shoreline to the Savior. The Lord says to you just as He said to Peter, *Follow Me. Be My disciple. Let Me turn you into a fisher of men. Let Me use you to change the world.* We never know what such a life will bring, but whatever happens we have Christ beside us, with all His wisdom for each moment.

Think of what Peter would have missed if he'd stayed behind mending his nets. Think of what Andrew would have lost if he'd remained with his boats. If James and John hadn't left their nets to follow Christ, we'd never have heard from them, and our Bibles would be missing the gospel of John, the books of 1, 2, and 3 John, and Revelation.

Think of what you'll miss if you don't become His disciple, His learner.

When Jesus said, "Follow Me, and I will make you fishers of men," that call is addressed to you as personally as it was spoken to the original twelve. Adding knowledge to your life begins when you leave the shore-line of your own purposes and become a disciple of the Savior. You have to say, "Dear Lord, I know You have a plan for my life, and I don't know all the details. But I want to follow You, whatever that means. I want to be Your disciple."

That's the attitude of a disciple. And it's the beginning of knowledge.

MOVE FROM HEAD KNOWLEDGE TO HEART KNOWLEDGE

In a similar way, discipleship means we move from head knowledge to heart knowledge. Head knowledge is vitally important. God gave us brains for a reason, and He has a lot for us to learn mentally, intellectu-ally, biblically, and doctrinally. But when Peter used the words *know* and *knowledge*, he understood knowing as a very intimate and personal con-cept that sunk its anchor deeply into the regions of the heart. This kind of knowledge makes you yearn for the Savior and grow in your love for Him. Philippians 1:9 alludes to this when Paul wrote, "This I pray, that your love may abound still more and more in knowledge."

When love and knowledge get together, it's a merging of heart and head.

Dr. Rosalind Picard is credited with starting an entire branch of engineering science known as affective computing, but don't ask me to explain it. All I can say is she's a respected academic voice in modern technology. But what I most admire about her is her knowledge. I'm not talking about her IQ or degrees, but about her journey from atheism to belief in Jesus Christ.

In high school Rosalind decided to be an atheist because, she said, "I believed smart people didn't need religion." She considered people who believed in God "uneducated," led debates in favor of the case for atheis-tic evolution, and dismissed those who didn't agree with her.

One night Rosalind babysat for a doctor and his wife. As they paid her at the end of the evening, they invited her to church. Rosalind was surprised because this couple didn't seem uneducated at all, but very sharp. Rosalind begged off, but eventually she accepted their suggestion to read the Bible, specifically the book of Proverbs.

"When I first opened the Bible . . . I expected to find phony miracles, made-up creatures, and assorted gobbledygook. To my surprise, Proverbs was full of wisdom. I had to pause while reading and *think*."

Rosalind read through the entire Bible, and it intrigued her more than she could have imagined. She "felt this strange sense of being spoken to" and began wondering if there might be a God. Reading through the Bible a second time, she was conflicted. "I didn't *want* to believe in God," she said, "but I still felt a peculiar sense of love and presence I couldn't ignore."

In college, a friend invited her to church. Her knowledge of Scripture grew, and she made Christ the Lord of her life. "My world changed dramatically, as if a flat, black-and-white existence suddenly turned full-color and three-dimensional. But I lost nothing of my urge to seek new knowledge. In fact, I felt emboldened to ask even tougher questions about how the world works."

Today Dr. Picard serves Christ in her role as professor of media arts and sciences at the Massachusetts Institute of Technology (MIT). "I once thought I was too smart to believe in God," she said. "Now I know I was an arrogant fool who snubbed the greatest Mind in the cosmos—the Author of all science, mathematics, art, and everything else there is to know."[4]

The knowledge Peter recommended isn't simply head knowledge. It's developing a heart yearning for Jesus, longing to know Him personally—to be His disciple and follow Him through the twisting trails of life and all the way to heaven.

Perhaps as you read these words, the Lord Jesus is urging you to follow Him. He is walking along the shoreline of your life right now, saying, *Follow Me, and I will make you a fisher of men.*

Perhaps you have a head knowledge of the Bible. Like so many, you've heard a thousand sermons and attended hundreds of Bible studies. But are you a disciple of Christ?

True knowledge is very personal. It's an individual friendship and an ever-growing intimacy with the One who says, "Come to Me, all you who labor and are heavy laden, and I will give you rest. Take My yoke upon you and learn from Me, for I am gentle and lowly in heart, and you will find rest for your souls. For My yoke is easy and My burden is light" (Matt. 11:28–30).

I WILL STUDY YOU

Knowledge means yearning and saying, "I will follow Him." But when Peter spoke of knowledge, he was also talking about actively learning, doing something very mindful and thoughtful. In short, the Lord wants you to study Him.

Is the word *study* a scary concept in your life? You're not alone. I hear it often: "I did enough studying when I was in school," or "I hated school, and I still have nightmares about taking tests," or "Well, that counts me out. I never could concentrate on anything."

To all these concerns and more, my answer is the same: the kind of study I'm talking about isn't like anything you've done before. Studying the Lord as His disciple will feed your soul. It will heal, uplift, and excite you! Each step you take in studying Him will bring you new knowledge and understanding. Remember, the word *disciple* means "learner," and learners study.

After Peter and Andrew and the others left their fishing boats to follow Christ, He had a lot to teach them. They listened eagerly to His great sermons: the Sermon on the Mount (Matt. 5–7), the parables of the kingdom (Matt. 13), the Olivet Discourse about the signs of the times (Matt. 24–25), the Upper Room Discourse (John 13–17), and His other formal presentations. They listened to the messages He preached in the synagogues, the arguments He waged in the temple, the conversations He had with the multitudes, and the parables He told wherever He went. They often asked Him privately for further clarification, and He taught them personally, sometimes rebuking and correcting them. He was (and is) the Master Teacher, and they had so much to learn.

Jesus wanted them to know—to truly know—the Old Testament Scriptures. In fact, two of His disciples later said, "Did not our heart burn within us while He talked with us on the road, and while He opened the Scriptures to us?" (Luke 24:32).

When you become Jesus' disciple—His learner—He teaches you, and He primarily does so through His wonderful book, the Bible, which is the voice of Jesus, as it were, speaking to you. As you read and study the Bible, your heart should burn within you too.

Let me suggest two ways you can engage more with God's Word under the tutoring of the Holy Spirit.

STUDY HIS WORD AS A TEXTBOOK

God's Word, the Bible, is His great Textbook of Truth, packed with everything you need to know about life. It's a treasure trove of information inspired by God Himself—His words to be studied and probed and pondered. It's not possible to add knowledge to your virtue if you neglect the study of Scripture. That's your textbook for life! I love the way Ezra is described in the Old Testament: "Ezra had devoted himself to the study and observance of the Law" (Ezra 7:10 NIV).

Growing in the knowledge of God means devoting yourself to the study and observance of God's law and of God Himself.

There's much about the Bible and about God I don't know. I've been studying both for many years, yet I'm still learning. Every time I open my Bible I learn something exciting I've never known before. The same will be true for you.

Almighty God created the human mind and gave us the ability to learn. We can learn many things—science, math, literature, history, sports, hobbies. Some people become engrossed in particular subjects and spend their lifetimes studying them. Many of these pursuits are good, but nothing is greater than the study of God Himself.

Contemplating the Lord and learning of Him bring a unique healing to your mind. Doing these things inspires your thoughts and gives you a new perspective. As your mind is filled with knowledge, your heart is filled with hope, your spirit is infused with strength, your vision is expanded to eternity, and your perspective is imbued with common sense. Consistent study of Scripture stabilizes your emotions. As someone once wrote, "A Bible that's falling apart usually belongs to someone who isn't."

In her book *It's My Turn*, Ruth Bell Graham advised everyone to have a desk, even if its "merely a piece of plywood stretched across two sawhorses. But have a special place for Bible study that doesn't have to be shared with sewing or letter writing or paying of bills."

She continued:

> For years, mine was just an old wooden table between an upright chest of drawers and a taller desk. . . . But on this desk I have collected a number of good translations of the Bible for reference, a Bible dictionary, a concordance, and several devotional books. I also keep notebooks [and] a mug full of pens. . . . When we were in school, we always kept a notebook handy to take notes on the professor's lecture. How much more important it is to take notes on what God is teaching us!

She went on to say that if you have to clear off a space for studying your Bible, you're more likely to put it off. But if you have a place where your Bible is always open, then "whenever there is a lull in the storm" you can grab a cup of coffee and sit down for a few minutes of refreshment and companionship.[5]

You need the Bible in your life every day. So design your own system for studying Scripture. Of course, start where you are. But don't stay there!

What works for me is to have my tools for study in all the places where I'm regularly scheduled to be and to set aside a quiet place to study in each of those locations. Since I travel often, I also study a lot on airplanes. When I get on a plane, I have what I need with me. Thankfully, God has given me the ability to block out everything and focus on what I'm doing.

At the very least, set aside some time every day—even if at first it's only ten minutes—to study Scripture. And keep a Bible with you wherever you go so you can follow Ruth Bell Graham's advice to find refreshment and companionship when there's a lull in the storms of life.

Let me give you some good news. You may have heard that Christians no longer read their Bibles—especially the younger generations of Christ-followers. Yet according to a six-year study conducted by the American Bible Society and the Barna Group, Millennials who are born-again, practicing Christians love the Bible. In fact, they're more likely than their parents or grandparents or even their great-grandparents to read it multiple times a week![6]

Yes, in a sense, the Bible is the textbook for life, packed with information that's fascinating to study and critical to know. The apostle Paul told us, "Be diligent to present yourself approved to God, a worker who does not need to be ashamed, rightly dividing the word of truth" (2 Tim. 2:15).

STUDY HIS WORD AS A SURVIVAL GUIDE

But the Bible isn't merely a textbook like your chemistry book or the instruction manual for your automobile. It's a living book, a personal book, a love letter, and a survival guide to pore over within the context of your relationship with its Author.

When you're His disciple, the Lord Jesus Christ speaks to you through the Bible as clearly, personally, and practically as He taught Peter and the others.

Let me tell you about a teenager who learned this lesson. Aldi Novel Adilang of Indonesia was in charge of a floating fishing hut—a sort of house on a raft anchored offshore with a long rope. At night Aldi lit lamps strung around the hut to lure the fish. One morning he felt a jolt. The anchor rope had broken, and Aldi began drifting in the ocean.

"On the first day I was okay," he said. "I wasn't stressed or panicking. I knew they would send a boat, but I was worried it would have to turn back because the winds and the waves were strong."

One day turned into another. After drifting more than a week, Aldi grew alarmed. He had a month's worth of supplies, but then the month came and went with no sign of rescue. Aldi caught tuna, scanned the horizon for boats, and sang gospel songs. At first he cooked his fish, but when his gas ran out he was forced to eat his catch raw. He floated for thousands of miles across the Pacific, and each day he felt more desperate. Sharks swam around his raft, but the worst moment came when he ran out of water. He tried to strain seawater through his shirt, but it was still too salty to drink. Just when he thought all was lost, it rained.

After forty-nine days adrift, Aldi was rescued by a passing ship.

After his rescue, Aldi said, "There were times when I [was] crying and thinking about killing myself. When I was crying the only consolation I had was reading the Bible." On that raft floating in the ocean, Aldi read Matthew, John, Isaiah, Genesis, and Psalms. The Lord's Prayer became as real to him as it was to Peter or Andrew.[7]

To Aldi, the Bible wasn't simply a textbook to study but a survival guide to read. The Lord Jesus spoke to him in Matthew, just as Jesus spoke to Peter. Jesus spoke to him in John, in Isaiah, in Genesis. Those words were a mental transfusion of hope and courage to an eighteen-year-old adrift in the ocean.

You have the same guide.

God has given us a Book to guide us through life! Given in sixty-six installments—from Genesis to Revelation—every word was written by those who were borne along by the Holy Spirit. In 2 Peter 3, Peter continued exhorting his readers to pore over Scripture. He wrote, "Beloved, I now write to you this second epistle (in both of which I stir up your pure minds by way of reminder), that you may be mindful of the words which were spoken before by the holy prophets, and of the commandment of us, the apostles of the Lord and Savior" (vv. 1–2).

This is a remarkable passage, for here Peter put his own epistle and the other writings by the apostles—which we now call the New Testament—on equal footing with the Old Testament and told us to "be mindful" of them. That is, to immerse our minds into the study of this wonderful, inspired, truthful, infallible Word of God.

Adding knowledge to your life and growing in the knowledge of Christ involves a lifelong, passionate pursuit of the Scriptures both as a textbook for life and as a survival guide for the soul. As Peter put it in his first letter, "As newborn babes, desire the pure milk of the word, that you may grow thereby" (1 Peter 2:2).

I WILL OBEY YOU

We've seen that growing in the knowledge of Jesus Christ involves both following Him and studying Him and His Word. But there's another layer to the word *knowledge*: obedience.

When Peter and Andrew and the other disciples decided to leave their nets and follow Christ, they developed a yearning for His love.

To them, knowing Him was very personal—it was a relationship. They learned the truth He imparted to them, but for that knowledge to really penetrate their lives they had to turn away from their old patterns and obey Him. They had to learn His will and His ways. They had to begin walking in what the Bible calls "newness of life" (Rom. 6:4). And their knowledge included saying, "I will obey You."

BE PREPARED TO CHANGE YOUR VALUES

The more we know about God's Word and His will, the more it changes our lives. Our desires change to reflect His eternal priorities. Our behavior and habits change. Most of all, our attitudes and values change as we develop the personality of Christ and become like Him, growing in love, joy, peace, longsuffering, kindness, goodness, faithfulness, gentleness, and self-control (Gal. 5:22–23).

Texas Monthly told of a student named Jaelyn Cogburn who wore a T-shirt to high school one day with Matthew 4:19 printed on the front: "Follow Me, and I will make you fishers of men." That very day she met a foreign exchange student from Pakistan named Sabika Sheikh. The two became friends, and Jaelyn learned all she could about Sabika's Muslim beliefs while seeking to share Jesus Christ with her. Sabika had never met a Christian before. Every day the two girls lunched together in the cafeteria, and Sabika began visiting the Cogburns, who welcomed her into their home with great love. Soon she moved in with them and was given an upstairs bedroom where she hung a Pakistani flag. She attended church with them, and Jaelyn spoke openly with her about trusting Jesus for eternal life.

On May 18, 2018, Jaelyn had taken her seat in biology class when the fire alarm sounded. As the students filed out, police cars rushed to the scene with sirens screaming. Helicopters appeared overhead, chopping the air. A sense of panic swept over the crowd amid rumors of a shooting in art class. Jaelyn dashed toward the school but was restrained. Borrowing a cell phone, she tried over and over to call Sabika, but there was no answer. By midafternoon, the Cogburns learned Sabika was one of ten people—eight Santa Fe High School students and two teachers—killed by a seventeen-year-old shooter.

Jaelyn turned to Scripture to help her heal from the terrible loss. As she sought God in prayer, she felt Him leading her to become an exchange student in the Central American country of Belize. Her purpose in going there? To make a difference as a disciple of Christ.[8]

When we truly accept the words of Matthew 4:19 in our minds and hearts, it's the beginning of a life of influence, meaning, purpose, drama, hardship, and mission. In other words, it's the beginning of knowledge.

You simply cannot acquire the knowledge of God without changing your personality, your behavior, your values, and your habits in life.

BE PREPARED TO CHANGE YOUR VISION

As you grow in the knowledge of God, you see the world differently. You begin to see it as God sees it. You will see the future differently as well.

A whole new world suddenly opens up for us when we look at life through the lens of God's Word. "It's not only information about God; it's the voice of God in print," said Dr. Tony Evans. "It shapes how I look at everything and how I view everything. It's the grid through which I evaluate the good, the bad and the ugly in my life and in my surroundings. . . . I am totally consumed with its truth, its power and its Author."[9]

Dawson Trotman graduated valedictorian of his high school class. He was also student body president, chairman of the student council, and editor of the school annual. But Dawson's life wasn't as exemplary as it seemed. He battled a compulsion to lie and was involved in petty theft. He dated excessively, drank heavily, drove fast, and hung out in all the wrong places. On graduation night he got so drunk he had no memory of the evening.

Dawson's life tilted even further downhill after graduation. He dismissed dreams of college, lost his temper frequently, and swore until the air turned blue. One night he was arrested when he was too drunk to find his car. The police officer said, "Son, do you like this kind of life?"

"Sir, I hate it," Dawson replied.

He was frustrated enough to attend a church event where there was a Scripture memory contest. Dawson learned ten verses rather quickly, then another ten. One day shortly afterward he was walking to work when one of those twenty Bible verses blazed through his consciousness: "Most assuredly, I say to you, he who believes in Me has everlasting life" (John 6:47).

Dawson stopped in his tracks. "O God," he said. "Whatever that means I want to have it."

At that moment another verse flashed through his mind as if it were an immediate answer from heaven: "But as many as received Him, to them He gave the right to become children of God" (John 1:12).

"O God," he said, "whatever it means to receive Jesus, I want to do it right now."

His biographer said, "He walked on. Visibly nothing had changed. Yet everything had changed. . . . He was amazed at his changed outlook."[10]

Dawson Trotman taught hundreds of people to become disciples of Christ and to memorize and meditate on Scripture. His vision expanded to the whole world through his organization, the Navigators.

When the Word of God gets inside your brain, it gives you a vision to change the world. It shows you how, one step at a time, to add knowledge to your virtue. That is the essence of discipleship: I will follow You. I will study You. I will obey You.

Now, where is that Book in your life? Is it close by? Do you have it open? Are you reading it consistently, studying it seriously, listening to God's voice daily, and obeying Him at every point?

DOORSTOP—OR DOORWAY TO KNOWLEDGE?

Many years ago David Mazurek bought a farm in western Michigan, and with the farm he inherited a large black rock on a shelf in a barn. The seller told him it was a meteorite and said it came with the farm. Mazurek used it as a doorstop. One day Mazurek decided to show the stone to a professor at Central Michigan University. Turned out, it's the sixth largest meteorite ever found in Michigan, and its value is in the six figures.

"I'm done using it as a doorstop," said Mazurek, and he recognized the meteorite could "turn into a cushion for his golden years."[11]

I doubt you're using your Bible as a doorstop, but maybe it's a prop on your bookshelf. Or lying forgotten in a drawer. Or maybe you're not exactly sure where it is.

Go find it. Keep it near you. Immerse yourself in it.

God sent down His written Word, the Bible, and His living Word, Jesus Christ, to provide you with all you need for life and godliness. With all the diligence you can muster, add to your faith virtue, and to your virtue knowledge.

That's discipleship. And that's exciting!

And this is eternal life, that they may know You, the only
true God, and Jesus Christ whom You have sent.

—John 17:3

Chapter 5

PERSONAL DISCIPLINE

Draymond Green is one of basketball's star players, but his career has been marred by emotional outbursts, technical fouls, and trash talking. He's known for yelling at referees, arguing with officials, kicking his opponents, and squabbling with teammates. He's turned flopping—deliberately falling down and pretending to be fouled—into an art.

But recently Green met his match on the court. He was playing with his two-year-old son, Draymond Jr. The toddler was trying to throw a small basketball into a kid-size hoop. But that's not all he was doing. He was stomping around, mimicking his dad's emotional outbursts, and flopping with every shot. Green was stunned, suddenly seeing himself as he was, and he admitted he was disgusted.

For now, at least, this epiphany made a huge difference in Green's performance. His coaches, teammates, and fans feel like they have a new player. Reporters have noticed too. One from the *San Francisco Chronicle* asked who should get the credit for "Draymond Green's newfound maturity and self-control." The answer: a two-year-old.[1]

Now, if a child can teach sportsmanship and self-control to a famous athlete, what do you think we can learn from Simon Peter?

When he began following Jesus, Peter was a lot like Draymond Green. He was impulsive and headstrong. He squabbled with his teammates and argued with his Coach. One moment he acted like a leader, and the next moment he acted like—well, like a two-year-old. But Peter met his match with Jesus Christ, and it was our Lord who patiently, gradually brought Peter to a newfound maturity and self-control—something He can do for you too.

Near the end of his life, Peter revealed some of the lessons he'd learned. God's divine power, he wrote, has given us everything we need for life, and that power is conveyed to us through His promises that enable us to escape the corruption of the world and live above its lusts and allurements. But we can't be passive during the process. We must diligently add virtue to our faith. And to virtue knowledge.

And to knowledge, we must add self-control.

That's the next component in the chain reaction of character qualities that makes us fruitful and effective in life. Self-control is the fourth tool in Peter's backpack. It's the next logical step to a life of success and productivity.

Of all the chapters in *Everything You Need*, this one might hit closest to home. So go ahead and say to yourself, "Okay, it's true. I do need more self-control in my life. God has multiplied grace and peace to me, but with His help I must add another layer. Starting now, I must bring discipline into my life."

What habits come to mind? Where do you most need self-control? Is it your temper? Spending? Time management? Daily devotions? Your work habits? Your entertainment or viewing patterns? Your appetites? Maybe your tongue?

That was one of Peter's problems, by the way—his tongue. He often spoke without thinking. But look what happened! As God taught him the discipline of self-control, Peter's words became so powerful that we are studying them two thousand years later.

That's why self-control needs to be a priority in your life.

SELF-CONTROL DESERVES PRIORITY

A popular advice columnist in the *Washington Post* received a letter that said,

> Dear Heloise: For over twenty years, I've taught school and seen a number of policy changes that were enacted to help students but have had the reverse effect. Students come to class without homework and tell me they didn't feel like doing it, or hand in sloppy work with grammatical errors and terrible spelling. With poor grades and a lack of self-discipline, they'll never make it in college.
>
> How can we get parents more involved with their children? How can I stress the importance of spending time (NOT money) with their children?

Heloise's answer? "Parents need to put down the cellphone, turn off the TV and computer, and spend time with their kids. Our children are the only truly important thing we will leave behind."[2]

Can you imagine a more critical problem in our society, in our homes, and in our personal lives than the breakdown of discipline? If you don't teach your children the secrets of self-control, the world certainly won't. But how can you effectively pass along those skills unless you yourself have added them to your list of virtues?

There's a sense in which our every failure is a lack of self-control. Adam and Eve sinned in the garden of Eden because they yielded to the Devil's temptation. Cain killed his brother, Abel, because he couldn't master his anger. Moses had trouble controlling his temper too, and it kept him from the promised land. During the days of the judges, everyone did what they felt like doing—what felt right in their own eyes. One of the judges, Samson, was the strongest man on earth, but he couldn't control his passions. Likewise, King David's greatest failure was his lack of self-control when he lusted after a beautiful woman named Bathsheba. The nation of Israel was destroyed by Babylon after losing a national sense of self-control and spiraling into indulgence and debauchery during the days of the prophets.

In the New Testament, self-control is one of the main implications of the gospel. Jesus said, "If anyone desires to come after Me, let him deny himself, and take up his cross, and follow Me. . . . For what profit is it to a man if he gains the whole world, and loses his own soul?" (Matt. 16:24, 26).

What message did the apostles stress to new Christians in the early church? The first century was a time of unrestrained sensuality and sinfulness. During the days of the Roman Empire, every lust was magnified and every desire entertained. As people came to Christ from this pagan culture, the apostles wrote letters to them, exhorting self-control, self-discipline, and self-restraint.

The apostle Paul wrote to believers who lived in Rome, the very center of the empire, saying, "Let us walk properly, as in the day, not in revelry and drunkenness, not in lewdness and lust, not in strife and envy. But put on the Lord Jesus Christ, and make no provision for the flesh, to fulfill its lusts" (Rom. 13:13–14).

That's self-control—evaluating our choices biblically in accordance to God's will. Author and pastor Randy Frazee said, "Self-control is not only about the discipline to stop doing things that destroy us but also about the discipline to do the things that build us up."[3]

This doesn't mean the Lord wants to spoil our fun. He created us to experience life "more abundantly" (John 10:10). He has given us "richly all things to enjoy" (1 Tim. 6:17). But He also tells us to "test all things; hold fast what is good" (1 Thess. 5:21).

Self-control involves making everyday decisions as well as setting long-term goals. Think of it as a trade-off. You deny yourself an immediate indulgence in order to accomplish a higher-level, longer-term goal. It involves saying no when you'd like to say yes. Saying "enough" when you'd like to say "more." Saying, "I won't" when you'd rather say, "I will." It's thinking before you act, and it's controlling your appetites, your tongue, your temper, your thoughts, and your eyes.

Self-control is a make-or-break discipline. It's the difference between success and failure in living a godly life.

SELF-CONTROL DISPLAYS MATURITY

There's perhaps no other quality that displays maturity like self-control.

For four years, a young man named Amir Parker juggled the demands of serving in the US Army Reserve while studying at Bowdoin College in Maine, where he was captain of the track team. He also worked about twenty hours a week at a job on campus.

Parker grew up in Baltimore, where his father was a truck driver and his mother a hair stylist. From childhood he was surrounded by violent crime in his neighborhood. But he came from a good family, he knew how to work, and he understood self-control. His training and work with the reserve took up more time than he expected, but he served his country without neglecting his schoolwork and personal aspirations.

When the local college paper asked Parker how he handled it all, he answered, "I do have a social life, but when it's time to do work, it's time to do work. Sometimes you just have to switch off your phone, block out distractions, and focus."[4]

You know what I would call Amir Parker? Mature. He's a young man trained in self-control, exercising personal maturity, and making hard choices with a clear intention to achieve his goals. He's an example of the day-to-day maturity and self-control Paul was talking about.

On one of his trips to spread the gospel, the apostle Paul visited an island infamous for laziness and hedonism: Crete. Even one of Crete's own poets said, "Cretans are always liars, evil beasts, lazy gluttons," and Paul agreed with that assessment (Titus 1:12).

The apostle stayed in Crete long enough to share the gospel and start some small churches. But he left behind his colleague, Titus, to bring order and discipline to those churches and to the new believers on the island. Titus learned it was no easy task to develop maturity among islanders from such a pagan background. As he tackled his assignment, he received a letter from Paul with some ideas. We call this letter the book of Titus.

No surprise—one of its central themes is self-control.

Paul wrote, "For this reason I left you in Crete, that you should set in order the things that are lacking, and appoint elders in every city" (1:5). These elders, or local church leaders, needed to be "blameless, faithful to [their wives] . . . not overbearing, not quick-tempered, not given to drunkenness, not violent." Rather, Paul said, they must be "self-controlled, upright, holy and disciplined" (vv. 6–8 NIV).

In chapter 2, Paul told Titus to teach all the older men in the church to be "temperate, worthy of respect, self-controlled." The women, too, were to be "self-controlled and pure." Paul continued, "Similarly, encourage the young men to be self-controlled" (vv. 2, 5–6 NIV).

Then Paul wrote perhaps the most powerful words about self-control in all the Bible:

For the grace of God has appeared that offers salvation to all people. It teaches us to say "No" to ungodliness and worldly passions, and to live self-controlled, upright and godly lives in this present age, while we wait for the blessed hope—the appearing of the glory of our great God and Savior, Jesus Christ, who gave himself for us to redeem us from all wickedness and to purify for himself a people that are his very own, eager to do what is good. (vv. 11–14 NIV)

The entire book of Titus is about bringing the believers on Crete to maturity, which was impossible without teaching them self-restraint and self-control—qualities now available to them through the grace of God.

Crete is not so different from our world today. Don't live like the other islanders on planet Earth. The same grace that brought you salvation can teach you to say no to ungodliness, intemperance, and worldly passions. It can support you in living a self-controlled life of maturity as you wait for the blessed hope of our Lord's return. God wants to purify you to be a person who is His very own, who is eager to do good. And in that process, He wants you to become disciplined and organized.

SELF-CONTROL DEEPENS DISCIPLINE

In her book *Disciplines of a Godly Woman*, Barbara Hughes wrote about the day when, after two years of marriage, she happened to see her husband's prayer list on his tidy desk. Her name was at the top, and beside it were the letters D and O. What did those letters stand for? she wondered. Delightful and openhearted? Darling and optimistic? She puzzled about it for days. Finally, she asked him what those letters meant. What was he praying for her to become?

"Disciplined and organized, of course!" replied Kent.

That didn't go over very well. But as time passed, Barbara realized how important those qualities are. "Discipline for me and discipline for Kent are not exactly the same thing, we've discovered. Our personalities are different, for starters. My husband is a morning person, and I wake up with the evening news. He finds sanity in structure—a well-ordered calendar with no unexpected interruptions. I welcome interruptions and love the surprise of a drop-in visitor."

But, she said, while she enjoys her spontaneous personality, "Spontaneity isn't an excuse for me to ignore the importance of discipline. And discipline *is* important for my spiritual life. In fact, it is the path by which the good news of Christ gives meaningful shape to all the days of my life."[5]

Well put! The good news of Christ gives meaningful shape to all the days of our lives as He helps us develop self-control. By saying yes to self-discipline, you let Him open lots of other doors marked yes, and you nail shut the doors marked no that lead to the basements of life.

You see, true freedom is impossible without constraints. This may seem like a paradox, but when we abandon self-control and follow our cravings, what appears to be freedom becomes a form of servitude. We become slaves to our appetites. Like a hunting dog distracted by a squirrel, we chase enticing distractions that prove no more meaningful than the scratching of an itch. Once we establish a pattern of having those itches scratched, they itch even more. Soon that pleasurable experience traps us into repeating the same act over and over. We feel less pleasure each time, but we feel as though we lack the power to stop, even as we descend into the pit of addiction.

Self-control means imposing limitations so you can focus on your goals. Limitations don't bring confinement; they enable freedom. Playing any sport is impossible without rules. Artists paint within the boundaries of their canvas. Driving would be deadly without lanes, stop signs, traffic lights, and speed limits.

SELF-CONTROL DEMANDS STRATEGY

How, then, do you make progress in this? What's your strategy? You can't sit around waiting to become more self-controlled. You have to plan for it, work toward it, and fight for it. Let me offer some suggestions.

ASK FOR THE HOLY SPIRIT'S HELP

First, welcome the Holy Spirit's help. I've been impressed by how often the concept of self-control is linked to the Holy Spirit's work in our lives. This theme dominates the last half of the book of Galatians. The apostle Paul wrote, "I say then: Walk in the Spirit, and you shall not fulfill the lust of the flesh" (5:16).

Notice the order. The Bible does *not* say, "Don't fulfill the lust of the flesh, and you will walk in the Spirit." No, it's the other way around. You have to be filled with the Spirit each day so that you are under His control, and He will empower you to say no to the lusts of the flesh.

Paul went on to describe the works of the flesh—that is, the areas we've got to control and avoid: "Adultery, fornication, uncleanness, lewdness, idolatry, sorcery, hatred, contentions, jealousies, outbursts of wrath, selfish ambitions, dissensions, heresies, envy, murders, drunkenness, revelries, and the like" (vv. 19–21).

"But the fruit of the Spirit is . . . self-control. . . . And those who are Christ's have crucified the flesh with its passions and desires. If we live in the Spirit, let us also walk in the Spirit" (vv. 22–25).

How does this work? We have to say, "Lord, I can't control this area of my life in my own strength. I need to be Spirit-controlled. I need the inner strength of Your Holy Spirit. Help me replace the works of the flesh with the fruit of the Spirit today."

In one of his books, Randy Frazee described a conversation he had with pollster George Gallup Jr. during an all-day session at Princeton

University. The two men found a quiet spot in the gun room of the historic Nassau Club, and the subject of self-control came up. Randy started pontificating on how Christians just need to get their act together and be self-controlled.

George kindly stopped him and said, "Randy, you're not an alcoholic, are you?" Surprised by the question, Randy said, "No, I'm not."

"Well, I am," said George. "My father was also an alcoholic. When I took my first drink, something happened to me that likely didn't happen to you or many others. I was hooked and couldn't stop. Even as a Christian, I tried and tried and tried. I felt so defeated, and it was ruining my life. Then in a moment of quiet desperation, I heard Jesus whisper to me, 'George, if you never lick this, that is okay. I died for this struggle in your life, and I still love you deeply.'"

Gallup paused and said, "From that very moment I haven't had a drink. It has been over thirty years."

Randy realized he must add the idea of "through Christ" to his thinking: "I have the power, *through Christ*, to control myself."

He wrote, "Yielding to the love, grace, and presence of Christ in us is the only way we can be victorious. While not every Christian struggling with an addiction may experience the deliverance George did, the truth of Christ's commitment and deep love applies to all of us."[6]

The Bible says, "For the Spirit God gave us does not make us timid, but gives us power, love and self-discipline" (2 Tim. 1:7 NIV). For this reason, I encourage you to ask for the Holy Spirit's help and welcome His fullness in your life. Self-control is really Spirit-control.

ADJUST YOUR THOUGHTS

Second, adjust your thoughts and make your mind an ally in the battle for self-control. Let's go back to Simon Peter. Our key passage, 2 Peter 1:3–11, isn't the first time he mentioned self-control. This was a lesson he'd learned the hard way, and he brought it up often in both his letters.

In 1 Peter 1:13, he wrote, "So prepare your minds for action and exercise self-control. Put all your hope in the gracious salvation that will come to you when Jesus Christ is revealed to the world" (NLT).

The key to controlling yourself is to control your mind, which is where most problems with self-control begin. C. S. Lewis noted that Christians often unfairly blame their sins on the body and its appetites. But in most cases, the body obeys impulses generated in the mind. Sometimes the body resists the mind; it almost always hated its first smoke and first drink. It was the mind that insisted on continuing those habits, thinking indulgence was sophisticated or cool.[7]

Likewise, the right thoughts circulating through our minds empower our self-restraint. American psychologist Walter Mischel designed the famous "marshmallow test," which consisted of placing a marshmallow in front of a preschool-age child and giving the child a choice—a rather cruel choice, it seems to me. She could either eat that one marshmallow now, or she could wait a few minutes and be rewarded with two marshmallows.

Mischel learned that children who exercised self-control and delayed gratification did so by changing their perception of the marshmallow. They imagined it tasted terrible or that they didn't want it. Their self-control was largely an act of mind-control.

In following the lives of the test subjects, Mischel found that children who were able to delay gratification for a significant time eventually performed better academically, earned more money, and were healthier and happier in their later lives. They were also more likely to avoid negative outcomes such as jail time, obesity, and drug use.[8]

Mischel put this lesson to use in his own life. After he told his three-year-old daughter that he'd stop smoking his pipe if she stopped sucking her thumb, he struggled to keep his side of the bargain. The key, he found, was to replace his pleasurable smoking associations with the potent image of a man in a hospital. Whenever he wanted to reach for his pipe, he trained his mind to visualize a patient struggling to breathe, fighting lung cancer, or dying in a hospital bed surrounded by machines and instruments. That visualization broke his habit.[9]

Scripture repeatedly urges us to banish thoughts that cater to our sinful nature and center our mind on pleasing God. As Paul wrote, "Those who are dominated by the sinful nature think about sinful things, but those who are controlled by the Holy Spirit think about things that please the Spirit" (Rom. 8:5 NLT). And Solomon cautioned us, "Be careful how you think; your life is shaped by your thoughts" (Prov. 4:23 GNT).

The ultimate answer to guarding your mind is to set it on Christ and draw on His strength: "Since you have been raised to new life with Christ, set your sights on the realities of heaven, where Christ sits in the place of honor at God's right hand. Think about the things of heaven, not the things of earth" (Col. 3:1–2 NLT).

ACQUIRE NEW HABITS

I confess I'm not a fan of Stephen King's books, but I admire his self-discipline. From childhood, Stephen wanted to be a writer. He wrote his first story in his preteen years and sent one to a magazine a few years later. It was rejected. But he kept writing, and in the next several years he built an impressive collection of rejection letters.

Still, he kept writing.

King was twenty-six years old and struggling to support his wife and two children on a schoolteacher's salary when he received a telegram from Doubleday publishing. (He could not afford a telephone.) They wanted to publish his novel—a story about a girl with telekinetic powers—and offered an advance of $2,500. A check for the paperback rights soon followed, then a movie contract. The rest is history. King became one of the most successful writers of our time.

He credits his success to self-control. As he explained, "I write ten pages a day, without fail." He has stuck tenaciously to this discipline throughout his career, holing up in his office and allowing no interruptions, phone calls, or emails until he reaches that quota. King said he frequently has to force himself to write because he feels no motivation or inspiration. It's during these times that his self-discipline—ten pages every day—is critical to his success. It's what has enabled him to publish multiple bestsellers of such consistent quality.[10]

Self-control like Stephen King's may not sound appealing, with daily isolation, no interactions, no pleasures, and no distractions until a set goal is accomplished. But in truth, this is freedom to fulfill your potential.

Like so many successful people, King developed habits in his life that empowered his self-discipline. And a habit is simply a way of doing painful things less painfully.

For example, say you want to get in the habit of making your bed every day. That's a simple area of self-control, right? In fact, it's so important that Admiral William H. McRaven wrote the bestselling book *Make Your Bed: Little Things That Can Change Your Life . . . and Maybe the World*, using it as the cornerstone of disciplined behavior.

In the commencement speech he gave to the graduating class at the University of Texas at Austin, McRaven took lessons he learned as a Navy SEAL and broke them down into practical principles for everyday life. He told the graduates that if they wanted to change the world, they should start by making their bed each morning. That way they could begin each day with a task completed.[11]

Why not try this yourself, especially if you struggle with orderliness and clutter? At first, making your bed every morning may be painful, or at least a chore. You have to stop everything else, pick up the pillows, pull up the sheets, tuck in the linens, straighten the comforter—all at the very moment you want to be holding your first cup of coffee.

But after you've done it for a few weeks, you'll no longer think about it. You'll do it automatically. It will be your habit—and you'll start each day with better self-control.

Paul understood that the godliness every Christian desires can be achieved with the right habits. He told Timothy to "exercise yourself toward godliness. For bodily exercise profits a little, but godliness is profitable for all things, having promise of the life that now is and of that which is to come" (1 Tim. 4:7–8).

Start with a small victory over some troublesome area of your life. Then use that victory as a foundation to stand on while you conquer another area. After several small, individual victories, your habitual self-control will have increased. No longer will you depend on sheer willpower. Keep doing this, and the habit becomes second nature. That's when your life changes. One small step toward self-discipline puts you on the path to a life of self-control.

I want to underscore the importance of allowing yourself to start small. What does a small step toward self-control look like? Here are some ideas:

- Omit one unhealthy item from your diet for one week—a sugary drink, a candy bar, the white roll at the restaurant, or the bowl of cereal at bedtime.
- Read a page or two of a book each day.
- Clean out one drawer of your desk or dresser.
- Set your smartphone to go off at 1:06 p.m. (for 2 Peter 1:6) and spend a moment saying these words aloud: "I will add to my knowledge self-control."
- Or just this: Tomorrow morning make your bed.

AVOID TIGHT SPOTS

As you change and grow, your desire to be more disciplined will not go unnoticed. So be prepared for the Devil to attack you! His challenge may come through seemingly small distractions that deter you from your new discipline. Or it may come via colleagues or friends who are uncomfortable with how your changes pull you away from them. It could even come in one stunning event. You won't know when his attack will come, so prepare yourself.

You see, when you grow in spiritual maturity by adding self-control to knowledge, you're building a wall Satan cannot breach. And he doesn't like that. As a result, as much as humanly possible, avoid tight spots— the places and circumstances where you know your self-control will be challenged.

In his book *Atomic Habits*, James Clear "zeroes in on the science behind building good habits and breaking bad ones." One of his most enlightening insights involves self-control: "'Disciplined' people are better at structuring their lives in a way that *does not require* heroic will-power and self-control. In other words, they spend less time in tempting situations."[12]

The Bible said that a long time ago. Proverbs 16:17 says, "The highway of the upright is to depart from evil; he who keeps his way preserves his soul."

The apostle Paul added, "Avoid sexual immorality. . . . Avoid godless chatter. . . . Avoid foolish controversies" (1 Thess. 4:3; 2 Tim. 2:16; Titus 3:9 NIV). Remember, the concept of avoiding evil requires forethought. You've got to prepare for temptation before it comes. You may have to change where you go, whom you see, what you do, or when you do it.

A study of 414 participants by the University of Chicago showed surprising results about self-control. The study defined self-control as "'the ability to override or change one's inner responses' and to refrain from acting on impulses." The researchers expected to find that people with strong self-control would be more likely to realize their long-term goals but less happy as a result of their self-denial. The results were surprising. It turns out "people with more self-control were also more likely to be happy in the short-term."

To understand this finding, the researchers conducted a second survey. Here's what they learned: "Instead of constantly denying themselves, people high in self-control are simply less likely to find themselves in situations where that's even an issue. They don't waste time fighting inner battles over whether or not to eat a second piece of cake."[13]

They're not tempted because their self-control begins long before the moment of direct temptation. They decide in advance what they want and dedicate themselves so thoroughly to reaching their goal that other enticements are barely noticed. They're not drawn to environments where temptation lurks. This clarity gives them peace. Eliminating this conflict from their lives makes them happier.

If you're not in a situation where you can simply avoid temptation, don't wait until you're being tempted to figure out how to say no. Prepare yourself! Life will come at you, no matter how much you'd like to believe it won't. The mind that prepares in advance builds a rampart against temptation. So exercise self-control in advance by creating a plan for how you will overcome temptation when it comes. Then, when you find yourself in such a situation, you'll already be strong.

As Mark Twain said, "It is easier to stay out than get out."[14]

ACCEPT THE PROCESS

Finally, if you *mess* up, don't *give* up. Learning self-control is a process. You won't master it all at once. Tell yourself, "I'm never going to give up or give in until I gain mastery over that issue by God's grace." Proverbs 24:16 says, "For though the righteous fall seven times, they rise again" (NIV).

Ruthanne Garlock, in her book *You Can Break That Habit and Be Free*, shared the story of her friend Peggy, who had a terrible habit of criticizing others. She held everyone to an impossibly high standard. And when they didn't live up to her expectations, she let them know.

"I was so busy keeping pace with a home, husband, three children and volunteer work, I seldom had time to enjoy life," she said. "Trying to follow up on everyone's work to put things in apple-pie order, whether at home, at church or in my children's schools, exhausted me."

When Peggy began realizing how judgmental she was, she resolved to change. But being critical wasn't an easy habit to break. Time and again, she'd be pleasant for a few days, then at the worst possible moment, criticism flew from her mouth like a dagger.

One day her husband questioned whether she even liked him. "I married you, didn't I?" Peggy snapped. That's when she realized she had to do more.

A book on conflict resolution helped. It suggested she explain her annoyance to others, acknowledging the problem wasn't in them but in her. At home she began taking responsibility for her negative reactions, calmly telling family members how she felt instead of nursing inner criticism.

For example, when Peggy's husband didn't show up on time, she later shared with him the panic she'd felt as a child when she was separated from her parents. It was an enlightening conversation that brought the two closer. Gradually Peggy was making progress in her family circle, but she was having less success outside the home.

One day at church her pastor preached about the difference between Christians who are simply immature and those who are rebellious. That was an eye-opener for Peggy. Her grumbling, complaining, and judgmental attitude violated multiple Scripture passages that warned against those habits.

Determined to overcome her critical spirit, she confessed to God whenever she felt it rising within her. Armed with Scripture and a deep commitment to improve, Peggy finally gained self-control over her attitude with God's help. To her surprise, the greatest beneficiary was herself!

"It's very liberating not to always be criticizing others and trying to fix every problem," she said. "I just refuse to entertain those critical thoughts that still come knocking at the doorway of my mind, and I release other people to God."[15]

Even if it takes the rest of your life to maintain self-control over some frustrating area, keep working at it. Keep pressing on, and the Lord will give you the victory.

 ## WHERE DO I START?

No wonder Peter included the concept of self-control in the middle of his list. Self-control deserves priority, displays maturity, and demands strategy. If you're not sure what area to tackle as you seek to grow in this area, ask your husband, wife, child, coworker, or friend. Say, "I know I need more self-control and personal discipline in my life. You know me. Where should I begin? What area in my life needs it the most?"

Of course, you probably already know what they'll say. So go ahead and get started, and never let up. Few things are more sobering than someone whose life is marred by a catastrophic failure of self-control.

Remember Boris Becker? At one time he was on top of the tennis world, a man of intense training and self-control who was still a teenager when he won the first of his six major titles. By age twenty-two, he'd won at Wimbledon, the US Open, and the Davis Cup. His career was stellar, and his house was filled with trophies.

Unfortunately, Becker's personal discipline and self-control didn't transfer from tennis to the rest of his life. He reportedly became so distracted by a girlfriend that he lost at Wimbledon to an unknown player. He gambled. He cheated on his wife. He went in and out of relationships, and his post-tennis life has been so void of discipline and self-control that he's filed for bankruptcy.

As I'm writing this chapter, his treasured tennis trophies and memorabilia are about to be up for auction, including the certificate commemorating his win at the 1992 Barcelona Olympics. Even his famed sweaters, wristbands, and socks are on the auction block.

How ironic! How instructive! Through his training and hard work, Boris Becker filled his home with trophies. But now, through his own admitted lack of discipline and self-control, the trophies will soon be gone—auctioned away to people wanting a small piece of the man he once was.[16]

But what if you're someone who already has pretty good self-control? If this is you, then congratulations, but don't assume you'll never be tested. God provides this precious trait in abundance so that when hard times come you can lean on His strength to achieve greater self-control than you ever thought possible.

When her grandmother's death left her family $4 million in real estate debt, twenty-six-year-old Paige Panzarello had to act. So she took charge and . . . waited for the mail.

"Every time a bill came, I called that person and said, 'Please meet with me and help me figure this out. If you give me time, I'll pay you in full,'" Paige recalls.

Three years later the entire debt was paid. Armed with her new knowledge of real estate, Paige started her own construction business. By 2006, she'd built a $20 million company and was the biggest employer in her county.

Then the recession hit.

One after another, her customers filed bankruptcy. When they didn't pay her, she couldn't pay her bills. Advisors counseled her to file bankruptcy too. But she knew that would only pass on the burden, putting many people who'd trusted her out of business. So she made the decision to sell everything she owned to pay her bills.

Once again, Paige went to her creditors and asked them to work with her. And once again, over time, she paid them all.

"I knew I was doing the right thing, but many days it was still hard to get out of bed. I needed prayer and I needed God. I put my decision into action by the grace of God. There was strength in me from Him that I hadn't known was there."

When the last person was paid, Paige moved in with her mother and started over. Today she's a successful real estate entrepreneur, and she calls the whole experience a blessing. "I'm proud that I did what I thought was right. And since then, God has given me one amazing blessing after another."[17]

It would have been so easy for Paige Panzarello to file for bankruptcy. To keep her beautiful home, her cars, her own material possessions. But through prayer and self-control, she took a different route, and stayed true to her faith and convictions.

To accomplish anything extraordinary you must blend desire for the goal with the will to take action to achieve it. This is how you commit to making yourself do what's right, whether you feel like it or not. The key is self-control.

The Bible clearly makes this virtue a priority to be developed fully in the lives of authentic Christians. It's a make-or-break discipline, the difference between success and failure in living a godly life. And remember, when you resolve to tackle those areas of your life needing greater discipline by leaning on God's power and promises, you'll find you have everything you need to become a person of self-control.

Better to be patient than powerful; better to
have self-control than to conquer a city.

—*PROVERBS 16:32 NLT*

Chapter 6

RELENTLESS DETERMINATION

At the 1983 Australian Ultramarathon—a footrace of 544 grueling miles from Sydney to Melbourne—an odd competitor showed up. Everyone else was a highly trained, commercially sponsored professional. But Cliff Young was a sixty-one-year-old farmer. Unlike the others, who were clad in professional running shoes and cool athletic gear with sponsored logos, Cliff wore a loose white shirt flopping over baggy overalls. He had rubber galoshes over his boots and a white baseball cap hung with sun-screening flaps.

The officials laughed, thinking they were being set up for a joke. But Cliff was serious and ready to run. His name went down on the roster, and someone pinned a number on his faded overalls. Uncertainty about Cliff continued as the runners lined up to start the race. Was this old man really going to compete against young, highly trained athletes with sculpted bodies? Some still thought it was a joke. Others thought him naïve or perhaps a little deranged. Some jeered and shouted insults.

When the starting gun fired, the runners took off. The crowd laughed at the contrast between the young contestants' disciplined strides and Cliff's odd-gaited shuffle. But five days, fifteen hours, and four minutes later, no one was laughing. Cliff Young crossed the Melbourne finish line almost ten hours ahead of the second-place runner. The astounded press descended on him en masse. How did this aging farmer accomplish such a spectacular run?

Two facts emerged: First, as a shepherd too poor to own a horse, Cliff often herded entire flocks of sheep alone, sometimes running day and night to keep up with the flock. Second, he didn't realize that runners in ultramarathons stopped at night to rest. He ran the entire distance without sleeping.[1]

Cliff Young had the primary attribute required to win any long-distance race: perseverance. He just kept on going. While his competitors eased their ordeal with rest, he relentlessly pushed through his exhaustion. His eyes were on the goal—and nothing else.

The apostle Peter listed perseverance as the next virtue we must cultivate to live the authentic Christian life: "Add to your faith virtue, to virtue knowledge, to knowledge self-control, to self-control perseverance" (2 Peter 1:5–6). The word *perseverance* literally means "to bear up under." It describes someone who remains steadfast in the face of severe trials, obstacles, and suffering.[2]

Perseverance is a never-give-up attitude, a commitment to move forward when everything is conspiring to hold you back. No matter what happens, you finish the job. Think of the English word itself: *persevere*. The prefix *per* conveys the idea of "through," so perseverance is the ability to go through a severe time.

Perseverance turns ordeals into opportunities. It gives us the opportunity to finish what we begin, to outlast pain and sorrow, to strive until we accomplish things that are difficult, and to demonstrate God's grace in all the seasons of life.

As Eugene Peterson wrote, "Perseverance is not resignation, putting up with things the way they are, staying in the same old rut year after year after year, or being a doormat for people to wipe their feet on. Endurance is not a desperate hanging on but a traveling from strength to strength. . . . Perseverance is triumphant and alive."[3]

THE FORCE OF PERSEVERING

Those who learn to persevere are forces to be reckoned with. In a world where most people give up and give out, those who keep going will accomplish more than they can imagine.

In Luke 8, Jesus told a parable about four different soils. The sower threw out his seed, and some of it, Jesus said, fell on good soil where it germinated. Jesus was actually speaking about the heart of someone who embraced the gospel message. Notice the way He put it: He said the good soil "stands for those with a noble and good heart, who hear the word, retain it, and *by persevering* produce a crop" (v. 15 NIV).

Perseverance has the power to accomplish a remarkable harvest through the person possessing it. It adds forcefulness and fortitude to our personalities, and it enables us to reap the harvest, gain the victory, finish the race, and glorify the Lord.

Byron Janis, a world-class concert pianist, played with the world's top orchestras and recorded many albums. From early childhood he studied with elite teachers and practiced for hours every day. Audiences marveled at the grace and nimbleness of his fingers as they flew across the keyboard, bringing to life the classical repertoire's most difficult pieces.

In 1973, at the peak of his career, Janis noticed a creeping stiffness in his fingers. After several tests, doctors gave him the devastating diagnosis: he had severe psoriatic arthritis in both hands and wrists. The prognosis was bleak. His fingers would become stiff as wood and severely crippled.

When arthritis fused joints in nine of his fingers, it appeared his concert career was over. But Janis was determined to challenge this. Without revealing his disease to the public, he spent long hours adapting his playing technique to this new reality. He relied on regular medications, acupuncture, ultrasound, and even tried hypnosis to cope with the pain. His wife, Maria (daughter of actor Gary Cooper), learned and applied a therapeutic massage technique to restore flexibility to his joints.

Janis continued playing for twelve more years, keeping the state of his health private. The world learned of his condition when he disclosed it at a 1985 White House concert. Despite several more surgeries on his hands, Janis continued to play the piano and became an active fundraiser for the Arthritis Foundation. He credits hope and perseverance for his success in overcoming his severe trial. As he put it, "I have arthritis, but it does not have me."[4]

In this fallen world, trials and suffering are inescapable. And they don't go away when we become Christians. The good news is perseverance can transform our curses into blessings. As Janis said in an interview, "Arthritis has taught me to look inside myself for new sources of strength and creativity. It has given my life a new intensity."[5] In other words, it made Byron Janis a force to be reckoned with.

Adding perseverance to the patterns of your life has more benefits than you can imagine, but the impact can be summarized in two broad categories.

PERSEVERANCE PRODUCES TRUST

The Old Testament patriarch Job is probably history's best-known sufferer. For much of his life, he was an exemplary, godly man with extravagant wealth and a large family. That all changed one day when Satan targeted him for attack. In a series of mind-numbing disasters,

Satan destroyed his wealth, servants, and children—all in a single day. Then the Devil struck Job with a painful and disfiguring disease. Job was reduced to groveling in ashes and scraping his sores with a pottery shard. His friends came to analyze his problems, but they did more harm than good.

Despite all this, Job never gave up. He maintained his trust in God, who showed up at the end of the book out of a whirlwind and restored Job to a place of unparalleled blessing. Job persevered through forty chapters of suffering, then Job 42:12 says, "Now the LORD blessed the latter days of Job more than his beginning."

The New Testament writer James said, "As you know, we count as blessed those who have persevered. You have heard of Job's perseverance and have seen what the Lord finally brought about. The Lord is full of compassion and mercy" (James 5:11 NIV).

God rewarded Job's perseverance and gave him double of everything he had before. The restoration of Job's wealth and family was the obvious blessing, but I believe there was another blessing that was perhaps even greater.

Job learned that the God who is big enough to control all facets of the universe is certainly able to direct the paths of His people. As Job confessed at the end of his story, "I know that You can do everything, and that no purpose of Yours can be withheld from You" (42:2). He learned to trust in God rather than question Him.

That, my friend, is an enormous blessing.

Perseverance is our willingness to wait on God to apply His grace to our frustrations and His answers to our questions. And as we wait, we continue to move forward. This is no easy lesson to learn, but the relief of learning it is one of life's greatest comforts.

In her book *You Are Not Alone*, Dena Yohe wrote about the pain of dealing with a suicidal, addicted, depressed, and self-harming daughter. Her book has been an enormous help to many worried parents, because she's very honest about the prolonged pain of having a child in crisis. One of the hardest things is realizing "this journey might not be over quickly."

Dena said, "How I hoped it would, but lowering expectations helped me to be more patient with the process, especially when we experienced setbacks." But, she said, she found great comfort in repeating a simple phrase: *I can't. God can. I think I'll let Him.*[6]

A lot of tough non-Christians have tenacity and resilience, and we admire them for that. But the kind of perseverance the Bible advocates is only possible with God. We have to wait on Him and give Him time to work His will into our situations. We keep going because when we can't, He can—and we should let Him. Doing so leaves a legacy long remembered.

PERSEVERANCE PRODUCES TRANSFORMATION

The second force that enters our lives through perseverance involves the transformation of our character. As we press forward, we learn so much along the way. In fact, the Bible teaches in both Romans and James that perseverance is at the heart of a mature personality.

Romans 5:3–4 tells us to rejoice in our sufferings, because "we know that suffering produces perseverance; perseverance, character; and character, hope" (NIV).

The book of James echoes that insight, saying, "Consider it pure joy, my brothers and sisters, whenever you face trials of many kinds, because you know that the testing of your faith produces perseverance. Let perseverance finish its work so that you may be mature and complete, not lacking anything" (James 1:2–4 NIV).

In other words, perseverance is the essence of maturity. If you can't persevere, you won't mature. We face trials because God wants us to learn to trust Him and to press on with grit and grace—that's perseverance.

Spiritual transformation doesn't just happen. It's forged through the fire of difficulty. When we maintain our trust in God despite difficulty or disaster, it produces a strength of conviction, ethics, courage, and rectitude that Paul summed up in Romans 5 as *character*.

History records many examples of people deliberately inflicting pain on themselves to achieve character. Medieval penitents whipped themselves or wore nail-studded devices that punctured their skin. Certain tribes of Native Americans suspended their warriors by hooks inserted into their pectoral muscles. Eastern mystics walked barefoot over hot coals.

But here's a secret I've learned over my lifetime: you don't need to go searching for trials! The world is well-stocked with an abundant supply. If yours haven't arrived yet, be patient. They're on the way. And when those tough circumstances assail you, don't run or hide from reality. Instead, face them head-on. Persevere through them, and you'll experience the mercy and compassion of the Lord, which will form in you strength of character and a heart that hopes.

Chris Tiegreen wrote,

Technological advancement has made travel, communication, and daily chores incredibly time-efficient, if not instantaneous. The result is that we're not trained in perseverance. We're not accustomed to pains that can't be relieved and problems that can't be corrected. When they come, we send up prayers with almost the same expectation as when we press the buttons on our microwave. A few seconds, we think, and we should be done with it. God usually doesn't work that way. He is thorough and precise, and He will not be rushed. When He tries us in the fire, as He did Job, nothing can get us out. The time cannot be shortened and our growth cannot come more quickly. We must learn perseverance.

Tiegreen continued, "No one has ever become a true disciple without perseverance."[7]

THE FORMULA FOR PERSEVERING

God knows we need trials to form character, just as athletes need resistance to tone their muscles. In His relentless pursuit of us, He will not leave us in our comfort zones, where our spiritual muscles atrophy from lack of use. Instead, He exposes us to obstacles to strengthen our faith, humble our hearts, and refine our character. That's why Paul urged Timothy to "pursue righteousness and a godly life, along with faith, love, perseverance, and gentleness" (1 Tim. 6:11 NLT).

So, how do you pursue perseverance? How do you find the strength to press on when you feel like giving up? The next time you're close to giving up, consider these biblical strategies for pressing on.

PUT YOUR PROBLEM IN PERSPECTIVE

On a rainy night in 1976, six-year-old Omee Thao and her siblings were awakened by their mother. "They are here," she whispered, "and we need to go now!" Communists had invaded Laos the previous year, and Laotian Christians were no longer safe. Now the soldiers had reached Omee's village. With no time to pack food or water, Omee's family and others crept stealthily to the outskirts of the city, where guides waited to escort them to Thailand.

They slogged through nights of torrential rain, the flooded and muddy trail making travel difficult and miserable. In daylight, they hid under bushes from searching soldiers. They survived on roots and rainwater. Poorly shod or barefoot, their feet were bruised and bleeding. Days later, they began finding the bones of earlier refugees who died trying to flee.

After twelve grueling days, Omee and her family reached the Thailand border. An official attempted to extort money from Omee's mother and clubbed her to the ground because she had none. They were trucked to a refugee camp and herded with other refugees into a space the size of a jail cell. Their meager rations consisted of rice and fish. Several refugees starved to death.

Yet, despite these ordeals, Omee later wrote, "We rejoiced daily and, as followers of Jesus, thanked God for His protection over our lives. Despite the hardship, we knew we had to keep persevering and enduring, for we had the hope that others did not have."

After enduring the camp for two years, Omee's family received a letter from a relative who had reached the United States, offering to sponsor them for immigration. In 1979, they were flown to Appleton, Wisconsin. Life in America was hard at first, but Omee and her family had the perspective of the terrible ordeals they endured. They adapted, and finally achieved lives of peace and prosperity.

Omee earned a master's degree from Denver Seminary in 2015 and now serves in church ministry with her husband. As she wrote, "All the hardships I faced in Laos and Thailand God faithfully turned into blessings."[8]

The Bible tells you to look at your problems in light of eternity. The book of 2 Corinthians is Paul's memoir of a difficult ministry. In this letter, he was more honest and open about his hardships than anywhere else in his writings. Yet, even as he catalogued his deep suffering, his unconquerable spirit shows up on every page. In the fourth chapter, he gave us his great secret: "We do not lose heart. Even though our outward man is perishing, yet the inward man is being renewed day by day. For our light affliction, which is but for a moment, is working for us a far more exceeding and eternal weight of glory" (vv. 16–17).

Architects tell us nothing is large or small except by comparison to something else. Comparison is the key to Paul's attitude. Putting things in perspective, Paul realized he was trading temporary sufferings for massive, eternally enduring, perpetual joy and delight. In a similar passage in Romans, he repeated this point: "I consider that the sufferings of this present time are not worthy to be compared with the glory which shall be revealed in us" (8:18).

When you weigh the outcome against the cost of your perseverance, not only does perseverance become your first response, it comes to you more *easily*. The ordeal may wear down your body, but that body will wear down anyway through age. So the choice is yours how to proceed—and I don't know about you, but I'd rather burn out than rust out.

I've mentioned Joni Eareckson Tada in many of my books because her insights as a long-term quadriplegic have inspired me and millions of others. In one of her books, she wrote:

> Looking down on my problems from heaven's perspective, trials looked extraordinarily different. When viewed from its own level, my paralysis seemed like a huge, impassable wall, but when viewed from above, the wall appeared as a thin line, something that could be overcome. It was, I discovered with delight, a bird's-eye view. It was the view of Isaiah 40:31: "Those who hope in the LORD will renew their strength. They will soar on wings like eagles; they will run and not be faint."[9]

If you want to keep moving forward, learn to think of your problems from God's perspective. Instead of comparing your challenges to your own resources, compare them to God's great power, His eternal plan, and His divine love. See them against His infinite grace. The trials that seem so large to us are well within His ability to manage, bless, and redeem for good.

JUST TACKLE TODAY

In light of that, your job is to keep putting one foot in front of the other. Tackle life step by step. When God appointed Joshua as leader of the Israelites and gave him responsibility for leading them across the

River Jordan and conquering the promised land, He told him, "I will give you every place where you set your foot" (Josh. 1:3 NIV). In other words, you can't make any progress unless you go forward one step at a time, but every single step will be a victory.

You don't have to conquer your whole problem at once, nor do you need to accomplish your life's work in one day. God's plan is step by step, and you have to take life day by day.

Remember what Jesus said in the Sermon on the Mount: "Seek first the kingdom of God and His righteousness, and all these things shall be added to you. Therefore do not worry about tomorrow, for tomorrow will worry about its own things" (Matt. 6:33–34).

Listen to that! Your worry doesn't help, so just tackle today. God alone is in charge of tomorrow. Sir William Osler, who was one of the founders of Johns Hopkins Hospital, called this "living in day-tight compartments."

People in addiction recovery groups, twelve-step groups, or support groups dealing with grief and other issues know the phrase *one day at a time*. There really is no other way to persevere.

Gerri Willis is a journalist with the Fox Business Network. In the middle of her career, she was diagnosed with breast cancer, and at first she couldn't face the diagnosis. She reached out to one of her colleagues, Jennifer Griffin, who had beaten triple-negative breast cancer. Jennifer told her, "Prepare yourself for the long haul."

In other words, get ready to persevere—to go through severe circumstances.

Gerri's experiences with treatment left her "horrified, shaking like a leaf." But she wouldn't give up. In 2017, she wrote an article about the benefits she's gained through her experience. "No lesson was more important than this," she wrote. "I learned to take life day by day and hour by hour."[10]

I've battled cancer too and had many other problems in life. I want to tell you from my heart that if you're going through a difficult personal trial, the words of Jesus contain great power: "Do not worry about tomorrow." Just take things day by day, hour by hour, moment by moment, and step by step. Put one foot in front of the other and keep going. The Lord will be with you, and He will secure every place where the sole of your foot treads. He will open up the future for you, and He'll get you there in His good timing.

Just tackle today with Him.

SURROUND YOURSELF WITH ENCOURAGERS

Peter Rosenberger has been caring for his disabled wife for many years, and his ministry to other caregivers has been of great help to thousands. In his book *Hope for the Caregiver*, Rosenberger pointed out that loneliness is the first thing that, in God's eyes, was not good. Many people who are caregivers become isolated. "Regardless of the reasons, time has a way of filtering relationships, and the caregiver is left to fend alone without meaningful interaction outside of a bleak situation that, at best, stays the same for long stretches."

Rosenberger wrote, "There are many reasons for the isolation that caregivers feel, but the results are universally negative. Without positive human connections, everyone suffers."[11]

That's why the phrase *one another* occurs nearly eighty times in the New Testament. If you're going to get through a prolonged struggle, you've got to have some positive supporters to cheer you on, to pray for you, and to brighten the corner where you are currently residing.

When Julie and Dan McConnel learned they would be parents of Down syndrome twins, they were afraid. Julie was forty-five years old, and the couple already had four children. They faced a trial they had not bargained for. They had no idea how to raise Down syndrome children. What challenges would they face? What special needs would have to be met? Could they cope with the heavy responsibility? As Julie said, "You feel like you've lost the future you imagined you were going to have." They even considered avoiding the challenge by putting the babies up for adoption.

Seeking encouragement as they prepared for the births, the McConnels connected with parents of Down syndrome children through the Internet and a local Down syndrome association. These connections paid off. Other families offered much-needed encouragement and advice, particularly a Scottish family who also had Down syndrome twins. Greatly reassured, the McConnels abandoned thoughts of adoption. If this difficulty was to be placed on them, they would bear it and persevere.

When Charlie and Milo were born, their doubts evaporated. The McConnels fell in love with the delightful little twins, and there was no looking back, no regrets. Yes, life was more difficult. There were special medications, regular tests, and the twins' learning processes were slower and required more patience. But as Julie said, "You feel like this thing that's the biggest blow you've ever received in your life has suddenly become a tremendous blessing that you're so grateful for. . . . I have these children who are so remarkable and so unique and so special. I feel like I have them for a purpose."[12]

The credo of the modern age is, "I stand alone. I don't need anyone. I have within myself everything I need to make it in this world." But this isn't true. It never has been. As the McConnels drew strength and encouragement from others, so do we all. This is not merely a preference. Having others around us for support and encouragement when the way gets rocky is a real need. It's the fuel that keeps us going.

As Solomon wrote,

Two are better than one, because they have a good reward for their labor. For if they fall, one will lift up his companion. But woe to him who is alone when he falls, for he has no one to help him up. Again, if two lie down together, they will keep warm; but how can one be warm alone? Though one may be overpowered by another, two can withstand him. And a threefold cord is not quickly broken. (Eccl. 4:9–12)

KNOW WHEN TO TAKE A BREAK

Another ingredient in the formula for persevering involves taking breaks. Persevering doesn't mean we never rest. Jesus took intervals of rest during His mission on earth. God rested on the seventh day after creating the world and its inhabitants. To rest is one of the Ten Commandments: "Six days you shall do your work, and on the seventh day you shall rest, that your ox and your donkey may rest, and the son of your female servant and the stranger may be refreshed" (Ex. 23:12).

Rest is a principle built into creation. As this passage says, rest is refreshment. It restores the depleted body and mind. How often have you faced a dilemma, desperately needing a solution that would not come? One idea after another enters your head, but none works. Finally, in frustration you lay it all aside and say, "I can't deal with this anymore. I'm going to bed." Then the next morning when you awake the solution comes to your rested mind.

As Anne Lamott said, "Almost everything will work again if you unplug it for a few minutes, including you."[13]

With apologies to ultramarathoner Cliff Young, rest is not a lapse in perseverance. Rest is stopping to take stock, reorganize, and regroup to continue the battle. Rest turns your conscious mind off and enables you to refocus—to see the problem from a new angle.

More importantly, rest indicates trust in God. Overworking yourself to make things happen can mean you trust too much in your own resources. (Remember the mantra of our age—"I stand alone. I don't need anyone. I have everything I need to succeed"?) Your willingness to stop and rest is an expression of your mature trust in God. You can rest because you know He will take care of you.

In Psalm 3, David spoke of how his enemies had increased. But he was not worried. God was his shield, the One who lifted up his head. In the midst of his turmoil, David wrote, "I lay down and slept; I awoke, for the LORD sustained me. I will not be afraid of ten thousands of people who have set themselves against me all around" (vv. 5–6). Despite enemies assailing him, David rested unafraid, knowing God was his strength and protection.

CULTIVATE POSITIVITY ALONG THE WAY

I know there are times when your spirit struggles. But when the opportunity comes for you to laugh or be happy, embrace that moment. You can't be defined by the grimness of any particular situation. You are here to be defined by the reality of Christ in you.

Christians are not stoics who merely endure life with plodding patience. We are Christ-followers who persevere by faith in God's great and precious promises. Remember the context for all this: you have everything you need through Him who called you by His glory and has given you His great and precious promises.

More than two years ago, three firefighters in Wilmington, Delaware, lost their lives in a terrible fire in the Canby Park neighborhood. One of the heroes who perished was a mother, Ardythe Hope. She left behind a precious daughter, Ardavia, whom the whole Wilmington Fire Department, in effect, adopted.

Recently Ardavia was awarded a $25,000 Bridging the Dream scholarship, given to academically successful students who have overcome adversity. She is the first Delaware student to win this award. Her school counselor, who nominated her, said this about Ardavia: "For everything she's had to deal with, she's one of the most positive people I've ever met. Every day I look forward to see[ing] her. If you didn't know her situation, you would never know it by meeting her. She doesn't carry that, she doesn't dwell on it, she just looks to her future . . . and every day brings a smile and positive attitude to everything she does."

Ardavia also has a message to everyone who has lost a parent. "When it happened to me," she said, "it was a major setback, but I had to persevere. And I just want everyone to know it gets better. . . . I just want everyone to know they're not alone."[14]

You are never alone. Jesus Christ said, "These things I have spoken to you, that in Me you may have peace. In the world you will have tribulation; but be of good cheer, I have overcome the world" (John 16:33).

REFUSE TO QUIT

What if you just refuse to quit? Refusing to quit is the theme of the entire book of Hebrews. The writer was addressing a group of discouraged Hebrew believers, and the key text is in chapter 10: "So do not throw away your confidence; it will be richly rewarded. You need to persevere so that when you have done the will of God, you will receive what he has promised" (vv. 35–36 NIV).

Do you remember what Luke said about Jesus when the time came for Him to leave Galilee and travel toward Jerusalem, where He knew He faced arrest, torture, flogging, and death by crucifixion? Luke 9:51 says, "Now it came to pass, when the time had come for Him to be received up, that He steadfastly set His face to go to Jerusalem."

What remarkable words. Luke seemed to indicate that a look of unconquerable resolution came over our Lord's countenance—an expression that said, "There's no turning back. Let's go and do this."

Hiking the Appalachian Trail has become the lifetime dream for many people, but the two-thousand-plus rugged miles are hard to tackle in one summer. Most hikers who set out from Georgia to Maine never finish, often because of injuries. Jennifer Pharr Davis did it three times. On one hike with her husband, Brew, Jennifer suffered shin splints, hypothermia, and a major illness. Within two weeks of starting, she told her husband she wanted to quit.

"If you really want to quit, that's fine," he said. "But you can't quit now." He told her to eat, rest, take her medicine, and complete at least one more day. By the end of the next day, Jennifer had regained her strength and was ready to press on until she made it all the way.[15]

That's wise advice, isn't it? If you want to quit, that's fine. Just don't do it today.

THE FOCUS OF PERSEVERING

One of the most inspiring scenes of perseverance in recent memory occurred in February 2015 at the Austin Marathon. Among those lined up at the starting line for the 26.2-mile race was Kenya's Hyvon Ngetich, a favorite to win.

She was the leading runner for most of the race until her body began to break down with only two-tenths of a mile to go. She collapsed to the ground, unable to run or even walk. But she refused to give up. As spectators and medical staff cheered her on, Hyvon—with her eyes focused on the goal—crawled inch by inch to the finish line, completing the race in third place.

Afterward, the race director said to her, "You ran the bravest race and crawled the bravest crawl I have ever seen in my life. You have earned much honor."[16]

Another runner, Ramiro Guerra, said, "When you see something like that it's just another reason to say, 'hey, you know what, I'm going to go up and give it my all.'"[17]

As Ramiro Guerra reminds us, sometimes we need to look at someone else's perseverance to find the motivation for our own. And that brings us to the final secret of this virtue.

We've looked at the force and formula of perseverance; now let's look at its focus. To move forward when you feel like giving up, focus your vision on Jesus Christ, for He is the one who empowers and enables you to keep going. Perhaps the strongest text in the Bible on this subject is Hebrews 12:

> Therefore, since we are surrounded by such a great cloud of witnesses, let us throw off everything that hinders and the sin that so easily entangles. And let us run with perseverance the race marked out for us, fixing our eyes on Jesus, the pioneer and perfecter of faith. For the joy set before him he endured the cross, scorning its shame, and sat down at the right hand of the throne of God. Consider him who endured such opposition from sinners, so that you will not grow weary and lose heart. (vv. 1–3 NIV)

The entire ministry of our Savior was plagued with difficulty and opposition. During His forty-day wilderness fast, Satan tried to derail Jesus with temptations disguised as painless shortcuts to His goal. Throughout His ministry, He endured opposition, exhaustion, and misunderstanding. Near the end He vividly foresaw the horrors looming ahead and prayed in abject agony, with sweat pouring from Him like great drops of blood. Finally, He was falsely accused in a mock trial, brutally scourged, and nailed to a cross to hang for six agonizing hours as blood poured from the thorns lacerating His scalp, from the wounds in His hands and His back, and finally from the wound of a spear impaling His side.

And yet He persevered through it all.

The result? Forgiveness for us. The shattering of the gates of hell. And glorious resurrection from the dead. When we keep our eyes on Jesus, He gives us the spiritual stamina to run with perseverance, to endure, and to never grow weary and lose heart.

When you feel like quitting, just look at the cross. Look at the empty tomb! Look at His ascension into heaven. Look at Him there on the throne. Look at His victory. Look at His love for you. Look at His grace. Consider Him. Meditate on Him. Talk to Him. Draw from His Word.

And never give up.

> *May the Lord direct your hearts into God's*
> *love and Christ's perseverance.*
> —2 THESSALONIANS 3:5 NIV

Chapter 7

CHRISTLIKE CHARACTER

Nate Roman of Marlborough, Massachusetts, came home from work one spring afternoon to discover someone had broken into his house. But this was no routine burglary, because nothing was missing. Instead, the intruder had cleaned Roman's house top to bottom, spic and span. The rugs were vacuumed, the beds made, and the bathrooms scrubbed. Even the toilet paper was adorned with origami roses.

Roman called the police, but the evidence of the break-in had been—well, swept away. It was what you could call a clean crime scene. "It's funny now, but didn't feel funny at the time," Roman said. "I kept the toilet paper roses as souvenirs." He wondered if a cleaning crew had come to the wrong address. But if so, how did they get in? There was no good explanation for the incident. It remained a mystery.[1]

As you read this, you may be wondering how to get in touch with that particular intruder! But you don't need an intruder to clean up your life. One of the wonderful surprises about committing your life to Christ is discovering His cleansing power. He stands at the door of your heart

115

and knocks. When you open the door and invite Him in, He comes, as it were, with a broom and mop.

Jesus knows how to clean house. In the Gospels, He cleansed the temple (John 2:13–17), and the Bible constantly speaks of His cleansing power and His ability to purify His people.

Jesus is holy, pure, and sinless. As you grow in Him, He makes you increasingly like Him. As you progress in your Christian journey, you'll develop an instinctive yearning for moral uprightness, for the need for your inner life to reflect Christ's cleanliness of spirit. Put simply: we all need someone who can disinfect our hearts, clean up our habits, vacuum our values, sweep the dirt out of our minds, launder our motives, spruce up our attitudes, and tidy up our testimonies!

In his book *Soul Detox: Clean Living in a Contaminated World*, Craig Groeschel wrote,

> Several years after becoming a Christian, I reflected on all the parts of my life that God had changed. Rather than occasionally telling other people what I thought they wanted to hear—I believe that's called *lying*—I allowed God to make me a person of truth. Instead of sharing the latest rumors about mutual friends with others—I think that's called *gossiping*—I learned to hold my tongue.

One of the more stubborn stains in Craig's life involved his movie-viewing habits, but the Lord gradually helped clean up those patterns too. Craig wrote, "It's time to come clean . . . if you would love to detoxify your soul from guilt, fear, regret, and all the impurities that pollute your relationship with God."[2]

When you receive Jesus Christ as Savior, you're forgiven, made pure in God's sight, and given eternal life; but you aren't yet perfect. Growing in God's holiness is a lifelong endeavor. It's the process of godliness. But like all the qualities we've studied, it doesn't happen to us passively.

We have a part to play. The Bible says, "Therefore, since we have these promises, dear friends, let us purify ourselves from everything that contaminates body and spirit, perfecting holiness out of reverence for God" (2 Cor. 7:1 NIV).

Does that have a familiar ring to it? It's similar to what Peter wrote in the great passage we're studying, 2 Peter 1:3–11. Remember how the paragraph opens in verse 3? "His divine power has given to us all things that pertain to life and *godliness.*" Notice that word. God has already given you everything you need for a godly life. But then Peter told us in verses 5 and 6 to add to our faith diligence, virtue, knowledge, self-control, perseverance, and . . . godliness!

But before you accuse Peter of circular reasoning, remember our approach. God does His part, and with His help, you do yours. Your spiritual formation and growth are a joint exercise between you and Christ, with Him providing the multiplied grace. Your role is to diligently add the needed effort to grow in godliness.

WHAT IS GODLINESS?

What is godliness? As we discussed in chapter 1, godliness is simply becoming more like God every day, which is to say, it's you becoming more like Christ all the time.

I'm told a portrait once hung near the entrance of the Alamo in San Antonio. It was supposed to be of James Butler Bonham. However, Bonham died in battle before his portrait could be drawn. Since his nephew bore a striking resemblance to him, the nephew stood in for the portrait of his uncle so future generations could know what the man who died for freedom looked like.[3]

In a similar way, Jesus Christ is the earthly portrait of God. The Bible says, "No one has ever seen God, but the one and only Son, who is himself God and is in closest relationship with the Father, has made him known" (John 1:18 NIV). The book of Hebrews adds, "The Son is the radiance of God's glory and the exact representation of his being, sustaining all things by his powerful word" (1:3 NIV).

If God were to sit for a portrait, we'd see Christ on the canvas. If you want to know what God's love looks like, study Jesus. If you want to know how God thinks, read the sermons and sayings of Christ. If you want to know about the wrath of God, look at the righteous anger of the Son of Man. If you want to know any facet of God's character or personality, study the life of the Nazarene.

By everything He said and did and was, Jesus, who is God the Son, manifested and revealed God to us. In the same way, your job is to manifest and reveal Christ to the world by what you say, what you do, and who you are. The essence of the *Christ*ian life is to increasingly resemble Christ. Godliness is Christlikeness, and Christlikeness is godliness. As you grow in godliness, you become an increasingly accurate portrait of Christ for those who see you.

Adoniram Judson was America's first overseas Protestant missionary, and he spent almost four decades serving and suffering in Burma. When he was dying, his wife, Emily, sat by his bedside reading newspaper clippings that described his lifetime of work. Some compared him to Peter and Paul. Others compared him to the heroes of Christian history. Judson quickly had enough. He clapped his hands together, burst into tears, and said, "Do not read me any more of those clippings. I do not want to be like any man. I want to be more like Jesus."

So do we! But how exactly do we do that?

Peter didn't give us a further definition of godliness in 2 Peter, perhaps because he had already devoted his first letter to that subject. The book of 1 Peter is all about responding to circumstances as Christ did. Peter told us that Christ left us an example and that we should follow in His steps (2:21). Writing to people who were facing persecution, he constantly reminded them that whatever happened in life, they should arm themselves with the attitude of Christ (4:1).

One paragraph in particular seems to capture the essence of godliness—1 Peter 2:9–12:

> But you are a chosen generation, a royal priesthood, a holy nation, His own special people, that you may proclaim the praises of Him who called you out of darkness into His marvelous light; who once were not a people but are now the people of God, who had not obtained mercy but now have obtained mercy. Beloved, I beg you as sojourners and pilgrims, abstain from fleshly lusts which war against the soul, having your conduct honorable among the Gentiles, that when they speak against you as evildoers, they may, by your good works which they observe, glorify God in the day of visitation.

EXAMINING YOUR IDENTITY

Basketball great LeBron James used an unlikely word when describing the first time he met his hero, Michael Jordan. He said, "It was godly. I've said that over and over before, but it was like meeting God for the first time. That's what I felt like as a 16-year-old kid when I met MJ."[4]

It's exciting to meet someone famous, especially when that person is your hero. None of us is above being starstruck. Now imagine having that feeling about Jesus, and having it increase as you grow in spiritual maturity. Godliness only begins when you truly meet God Himself through Jesus Christ. That is a *godly* experience, and it's the beginning of *godliness* in your life.

This experience changes your very identity. That's why Peter continued his discussion on godliness by reminding us of who we are in Christ, and he zeroed in on three specific things.

YOU ARE GOD'S POSSESSION

Notice the first word of 1 Peter 2:9: *but*. That indicates we're breaking into a thought. In verse 8, Peter described the people in the world who reject Jesus Christ, the chief cornerstone. They consider Him "'a stone of stumbling and a rock of offense.' They stumble, being disobedient to the word."

In verse 9, Peter continued, "*But* you are a chosen generation, a royal priesthood, a holy nation, His own special people."

These phrases he was using to describe the followers of Christ have great meaning, for Peter reached back into the Old Testament to find them. These were concepts that described the nation of Israel.

In the Old Testament, God was effusive in declaring His remarkable affection to the nation who would produce the Messiah. Of all the people on earth, He chose them to be His own special people. He came down to live among them. He bestowed remarkable blessings upon them, and He used them to bring the promised Messiah into the world. They were His treasured possession.

God still loves Israel, and that nation still has a vital role to play in the future; but here Peter was deliberately borrowing this Old Testament language to describe you and me—the followers of Jesus.

I can't get over the power behind the phrase, *You are His own special people*. Peter was writing to those who were suffering, many because of their faith. Many lived in poverty. Some were slaves. Many were illiterate, and some were sick and elderly. But he said, in effect, "You are the most special people on earth. It isn't the imperial and elite who are special. It's you! You are God's special people, that you may proclaim the praises of Him who called you out of darkness into His marvelous light."

Let's make it personal. When you come to Jesus Christ, *you are His own special person*. To add godliness in your life, remember to Whom you belong! How can you live a godly life without remembering you are God's special possession, someone He redeemed by the blood of Jesus to be His very own? He called you out of darkness and into His marvelous light.

This lesson was a great help to Janet Holm McHenry, who speaks to women's groups across the nation. "I never felt special," she wrote, looking back over her life.

> I wasn't the smartest kid in the class—there were always others smarter than I. I wasn't the most athletic. The one swim contest I entered I got third . . . out of three. I also never thought I was attractive. Enough said. To matter in this world, I took on leadership roles to earn others' respect. In my senior year in high school I ran for and won SIX offices, including senior class secretary. . . . I thought I'd make my mark by DOING things. Instead, I only made myself exhausted.

Two years after graduating from high school, Janet learned she could have a personal relationship with Jesus and—this was totally new to her—she realized "HE wanted a relationship with ME. Like the Israelites I learned this scriptural truth: 'The Lord your God has chosen you out of all the peoples on the face of the earth to be his people, his treasured possession' (Deut. 7:6)."

The effect on Janet was astounding. "I am treasured," she wrote. "God values me and wants a relationship with me. He wants to delight me, inspire me, fulfill me, and walk with me, day by day."

In the years since, Janet tells people, "YOU are his treasured possession too. And if you're trying to find your worth in doing things or winning things or being the prettiest/smartest/most athletic . . . just STOP, okay? Just stop. Because Jesus loves you . . . and he is enough."[5]

YOU ARE GOD'S PILGRIM

One of the greatest concepts Peter used was the idea of being a traveler passing through life on the way to heaven. This wasn't original to him. Centuries before, when the king of Egypt had asked the patriarch Jacob his age, the old man answered, "The days of the years of my pilgrimage are one hundred and thirty years" (Gen. 47:9).

King David similarly said, "For we are aliens and pilgrims before You" (1 Chron. 29:15). And Psalm 84:5 says, "Blessed is the man whose strength is in You, whose heart is set on pilgrimage."

It was Peter, however, who really took this to heart and emphasized it to us. He addressed his first letter "to the pilgrims of the Dispersion" (1 Peter 1:1)—in other words, to Christians who were scattered by persecution but were traveling onward to heaven. In verse 17, he said: "conduct yourselves throughout the time of your stay here in fear."

Now, in 1 Peter 2:11, he pleaded, "Beloved, I beg you as sojourners and pilgrims, abstain from fleshly lusts which war against the soul."

This world isn't your home, and you aren't here for long. When you realize that, it changes your approach to everything. Your house, condo, or apartment isn't your permanent home; you've got a mansion in heaven. Your wardrobe isn't as important as you think; one day it'll end up in a rummage sale. Your prized set of collectibles will gather dust in a flea market. Your wealth isn't going to last; only what you send ahead of you will endure as you invest in God's kingdom.

You're a pilgrim, a traveler, a wayfarer, a temporary resident, and your real citizenship is in heaven (Phil. 3:20). You're not a citizen of earth going to heaven; you are a citizen of heaven passing through earth. It's necessary to keep reminding yourself where you're going and whom you're going to see.

Perhaps the most famous portrayal of this is John Bunyan's classic book *Pilgrim's Progress*, published in 1678. The chief character in *Pilgrim's Progress* is Christian, who found his burden lifted at Calvary, and then he set out toward heaven—the Celestial City. His journey contained many conflicts and discouragements, but all of them increased his grip on godliness in life. He was especially disturbed in the city of Vanity Fair, but he escaped the lure and lusts of the town and traveled onward with a new friend named Hopeful.

Throughout the book, Christian did what Peter said: "As sojourners and pilgrims, abstain from fleshly lusts which war against the soul."

Dr. Donald Whitney is a professor who has assigned *Pilgrim's Progress* to over a thousand students. He's written widely about the power of its images, especially the magnetism of the Celestial City. "If you read one of the world's all-time bestsellers, John Bunyan's *Pilgrim's Progress*," wrote Whitney, "you'll read the writing of a man obsessed with the Celestial City. One of the signs of becoming more like Jesus is increasingly wanting to be where He is."[6]

Wow! One of the signs of godliness is increasingly wanting to be where Jesus is. What a wonderful way to recognize your progress!

YOU ARE GOD'S PLATFORM

Peter continued, "You are a chosen generation . . . that you may proclaim the praises of Him who called you out of darkness into His marvelous light . . . having your conduct honorable among the Gentiles, that when they speak against you as evildoers, they may, by your good works which they observe, glorify God in the day of visitation" (1 Peter 2:9, 12).

You are the platform and the pulpit from which God proclaims His message to the world. This demands and develops your godliness.

Dr. Tom Catena is a physician who lives among the half-million inhabitants of the Nuba Mountains of Africa. There are few roads there, and most villages are connected by ancient paths. The people are caught in the middle of unspeakable warfare. They've been the targets of the Sudanese government's scorched-earth strategy. Villages and farms have been bombed, and residents have fled into the mountains, where mass starvation ensued. No one knows how many have died.

Catena, who is from Amsterdam, New York, is the only physician permanently stationed among the Nuba people. His hospital has been bombed eleven times, but amid the carnage you can see him removing shrapnel from the injured, amputating the limbs of wounded children, delivering babies, removing appendixes, and more.

The *New York Times* ran an article about him, and they took their headline from a comment made about Dr. Catena from a local Muslim man: "He's Jesus Christ."[7]

We don't have to go to the Nuba Mountains to remind people of Christ. There are needs all around us. When Hurricane Florence hit North Carolina in 2018, Daniel Blevins, who owned a cleaning business, took time off to help his neighbors. One of them told a reporter, "Daniel didn't even know me and Daniel showed me love. He reminds me of Jesus."[8]

Have you heard about the guy who started the Burly Man Coffee company? His name is Jeremy Wiles, and his company's slogan is "Be kind and drink great coffee." Jeremy is a follower of Christ, and he's disturbed by other coffee companies that support causes that don't correspond to his Christian values. His company puts its money into helping single moms in need. "As a Christian (company)," said Wiles, "we're supposed to be the hands and feet of Jesus."[9]

To grow in godliness, we have to work hard to maintain our own honorable conduct. Our attitudes and actions should be so sterling that even when someone tries to revile us, they'll have to admit failure—at least when Christ comes. We could paraphrase verse 12 like this: "Live such a godly life while you're traveling through the world that even those who criticize you will have to admit when Jesus comes that you were right and that your example to them was godly."

EXPRESSING YOUR IDENTITY

We've seen how godliness is the nature of our Christian identity; we are God's special people, we are His pilgrims journeying through this earthly life to reach our heavenly home, and we are His unique platform to reach the world.

Now that we understand our Christian identity, how do we use it?

Brian Rosner, the principal of Ridley College in Melbourne, Australia, was sitting in a car in northeast Scotland on a winter's day in 1998. The sun was setting, the wind was howling, and the temperature was freezing. As he waited for his windshield to thaw, Rosner adjusted the rearview mirror and caught a glimpse of himself. For a moment he felt as if he were looking at a stranger. He didn't know who he was anymore.

Rosner wasn't experiencing amnesia; he was feeling the impact of his life being upended. His wife of thirteen years had abruptly left him, and Rosner was shattered. He wrote, "Cherished memories seemed like they belonged to someone else. Half the photos in my mind's album went missing." The person he'd been was gone, and a large portion of his life had evaporated, melting away like the ice on his windshield.

Rosner turned to God and to the Bible, and he realized the traditional identity markers that often define us don't tell the whole story. We're more than our marital status, our occupation, and our possessions. We belong to God. The important thing is being known and loved by God. Our identity is in Him.[10]

In the years since, Rosner has thoroughly studied the subject of personal identity, and he believes we're in the middle of a global identity crisis that profoundly affects our world. Unless we forge our identity in Christ and anchor it in His love, we're adrift.

"Being known by God gives a person a profound sense of significance and value," said Rosner. "It provokes a needed humility, supplies cheering comfort when things go wrong, and offers clear direction for how to live."[11]

It's not enough to examine our God-given identity; we must also express it. Here are three ways to do just that.

GODLINESS IS ABOUT OWNERSHIP—LIVE LIKE YOU BELONG

Sadly, I see that loss of identity Rosner described everywhere I go. People today have lost their sense of belonging. Our world is fractured, with entire populations of humanity displaced. Our nation is divided, leaving many people feeling like victims. Our homes are broken, leaving people disconnected. At the same time, our electronic media and so-called social networks have further isolated us.

It's so serious that *Sesame Street* added a new character to its puppet lineup—Karli, a yellow-haired friend of Elmo's who introduces viewers to the concept of "for-now parents." Karli is there to encourage foster children. The show wants to give every child a sense of belonging.[12]

It breaks my heart to think that any child, youth, or adult would lose the sense of belonging so crucial to our well-being. That's why I love the gospel message that Jesus Christ can give you—the ultimate and eternal knowledge that you belong. The writer of Psalm 73 endured a confused time of discouragement and depression, but the reality that pulled him through was this: "Yet I still belong to you; you hold my right hand" (v. 23 NLT).

I have seen, more times than I can count, that the lasting antidote to this global identity crisis is Christ. Nothing in the world anchors and stabilizes your sense of self more deeply or positively than when you claim your identity in Christ and follow His clear directions for your life.

When you realize you are God's special possession, you think twice about the things you do, the places you go, the words you say, the feelings you harbor, the habits you keep, and the entertainment you consume. If we belong to God, shouldn't our lives be characterized by godliness? Yes!

The Bible says, "You are not your own. . . . Therefore honor God with your bodies" (1 Cor. 6:19–20 NIV).

Romans 1:6–7 says, "You also are . . . called to belong to Jesus Christ . . . and called to be his holy people" (NIV).

Romans 14:8 says, "If we live, we live for the Lord; and if we die, we die for the Lord. So, whether we live or die, we belong to the Lord" (NIV).

When you come to Jesus Christ, your sense of identity is bound up in Him. The one fact that determines who you are isn't your ethnicity, your gender, your background, your citizenship, your political party, or your social or financial status. It's only this: you are His special person.

The more you're with Christ, the more you want to be like Him. The more you study Him, the more you'll emulate Him. The more you love Him, the more godly you'll become. It's not a matter of five easy steps. It's a process of growth over a lifetime.

GODLINESS IS ABOUT CITIZENSHIP—
KEEP YOUR EYES ON HEAVEN

When I travel, I'm the only one in my family who refuses to change the time on my watch. Wherever I am, I want to know what time it is at home in San Diego. I started this habit many years ago so I could keep track of the important things that were happening at home—what was going on at the church or with my family. It is more important for me to know what time it is in San Diego than wherever I am. I don't change the time on my watch because it's a reminder of where I want to be.

Keep your watch on heaven's time—that's the most important time. The Bible says, "Set your mind on things above, not on things on the earth" (Col. 3:2). That's what we're supposed to do as pilgrims.

This was so important to Peter that he came to the end of his life with one thing on his mind: seeing Jesus again. In the last chapter we have from his pen, he talked about the return of Jesus to planet Earth.

He said:

> But the day of the Lord will come as a thief in the night, in which the heavens will pass away with a great noise, and the elements will melt with fervent heat; both the earth and the works that are in it will be burned up. Therefore, since all these things will be dissolved, what manner of persons ought you to be in holy conduct and *godliness*. (2 Peter 3:10–11 NIV)

Just as you diligently add godliness to your life by remembering you are God's special person, also keep in mind heaven—God's special place. Heaven is sinless, pure, perfect, beautiful, and radiant. The closer you get to heaven, the more you should reflect its characteristics.

Peter went on to say, "We, according to His promise, look for new heavens and a new earth in which righteousness dwells. Therefore, beloved, looking forward to these things, be diligent to be found by Him in peace, without spot and blameless" (vv. 13–14).

Here's the essence of the principle: you become like the place you're most wanting to go to and the person you're most wanting to see.

Imagine a child looking forward to going to Disneyland. They watch Mickey Mouse cartoons. They dress up like Disney characters. They listen to Disney music. They pretend to be in Disney movies. They sleep in Disney pajamas and play with Disney toys.

While I don't get excited about theme parks, studying what the Bible says about the return of Christ and my heavenly home thrills me! That's why I make no apology for preaching and teaching so frequently on biblical prophecy, the signs of the times, the end of the age, the return of Christ, and the glories of heaven. It's not just doctrinal curiosity. If you want to become more godly, keep focused on those truths. Study what the Bible says about the future. Anticipate the return of Christ. Set your mind fully on the grace to be given to you when He is revealed.

A woman who was facing the trials of growing old asked missionary and educator J. Robertson McQuilkin, "Why does God let us get old and weak?" McQuilkin thought for a moment and then replied,

> I think God has planned the strength and beauty of youth to be physical. But the strength and beauty of old age is spiritual. We gradually lose the strength and beauty that is temporary so we will concentrate on the strength and beauty that is forever. And so we will be eager to leave the temporary, deteriorating part of us, and be truly homesick for our eternal home. If we stayed young and strong and beautiful, we might never want to leave.[13]

This world isn't your true home. You're here for a brief time—a few hours, days, weeks, or years. Your eternal Savior is coming for you, and your eternal home is ready. To grow in godliness, think more about the return of Christ and the eternal joys of heaven. There's strength in reminding yourself that you are a pilgrim traveling through the world for Christ.

GODLINESS IS ABOUT STEWARDSHIP— CARRY OUT YOUR ASSIGNMENT

A steward is someone who represents an owner. He faithfully carries out the wishes of that owner, acting on his behalf, doing what he knows the owner would do in any given situation.

Paul wrote, "We are ambassadors for Christ" (2 Cor. 5:20). Think of it—you are an ambassador for Christ! What, then, is your assignment? It's to bring glory to God through your words, your deeds, your thoughts, and your actions whenever possible.

Even a ten-year-old can carry out his assignment for Jesus, and even in the face of terrible trouble. Xavier Cunningham of Harrisonville, Missouri, was playing with a couple of friends when they decided to climb into a nearby tree house. They didn't know the tree house was already occupied by a swarm of yellow jackets. The wasps attacked the boys, and Xavier tumbled from the tree. He fell facedown and landed on a rotisserie meat skewer the boys had found. The rod went through his face and head.

Somehow Xavier managed to get home, where his mom, Gabrielle Miller, was understandably horrified. With the yellow jackets still caught in his clothing and still stinging him, Gabrielle got her son in the car and raced to the ER.

"I'm dying, mom," Xavier told her. "I can feel it . . . I wanna see Jesus, but not right now."

Gabrielle had the wisdom to say, "Jesus is here with us."

Xavier ended up at the University of Kansas Medical Center, where a staff of one hundred assembled for the risky procedure of removing the rod. The skewer had pierced Xavier's left cheekbone all the way to the back of his skull, but it had missed his eye, brain, and spinal cord. The doctors marveled, calling it a one-in-a-million trajectory. The surgery was success-ful, and Xavier recovered while listening over and over to the worship song "Reckless Love."

Now, read these next words slowly, because it's hard to believe they came from a child. After his surgery Xavier said, "So when you're getting to know Jesus you're like, 'Oh, he saved us. He gave his life for us.' And after [something like this happens], it's just like he really truly is the God almighty."

The media called this the "Missouri miracle," and newspapers and television networks throughout America gave Jesus Christ the credit through Xavier's testimony.[14]

Whatever your age, your trials can become testimonies. Then, when you do see Jesus, you'll learn that your conduct among the Gentiles brought glory to God.

That's godliness.

MORE LIKE JESUS

For the film *Judy*, Renée Zellweger worked hard to become the famed actress and singer Judy Garland. If you've ever watched *The Wizard of Oz*, you'll remember Garland's remarkable voice. Millions of people thought she was as wholesome as apple pie because that was the image we were given.

But behind the scenes, Garland struggled with her self-image, the pressures of stardom, depression, and a spiraling addiction to alcohol and drugs. She suffered financial pressures, mental breakdowns, multiple marriages, and career upheaval. She became suicidal, and in 1969 she was found dead in the bathroom of a rented house in London at age forty-seven.

In preparation for the role of this iconic American actress, Zellweger poured all her energy into transforming herself into the image of Judy Garland. She "immersed herself in all things Judy." She read all she could about Garland. She took music lessons and learned choreography. She studied Judy's voice to duplicate it. She studied Judy's gestures, posture, walk, and speech patterns. She used prosthetics, contact lenses, wigs, and costumes. During filming, Zellweger sat in the makeup chair two hours each day to be transformed into Judy Garland.[15]

This is how you become like someone—you study everything about them and you emulate them. In the same way a great actress immerses herself in a character until she "becomes" that person, you can immerse yourself in Jesus to become more godly.

Yes, this takes work. It takes putting Him first and letting Him be Lord over everything in your life. Read all you can about Christ in the Gospels and keep reading His Word throughout your life. Study our Lord's walk and His talk, and repeatedly ask yourself that famous question: "What would Jesus do?"

If godliness is becoming more like Jesus, remember this: Jesus not only belonged to God, but He also *was* God and He belonged to heaven. He came to earth as a pilgrim to carry out an assignment only He could do, and then He returned to heaven to prepare a place for you so that you can follow in His steps to join Him.

And the more you walk in His steps, the more attuned you become to His will.

About midnight on April 25, Collin Dozier, age thirty-one, was driving home when he noticed an abandoned car on the side of the road on Lesner Bridge in Virginia Beach. Dozier felt he should stop and investigate. "I just felt the Holy Spirit speak to me and tell me to go up there," he said. When he walked onto the huge span, he saw a twenty-seven-year-old man, Jacob Palmer, getting ready to jump to his death.

"Hey, man, don't do it," Dozier called. "Jesus loves you. He's got a plan for your life." No matter what Dozier said, Palmer didn't respond. Still, Dozier kept trying. "Man, I've gone through a lot of hard times in my life and there's only one thing that's really going to help me get through those hard times and that's turning to the Lord."

About that time, the police showed up. Palmer, who was high on meth, PCP, heroin, and cocaine, grew more agitated. Dozier remembers him saying, "Leave me alone. I have a gun. I'm going to kill you both, there's going to be two murders tonight if you don't leave me alone right now."

Palmer was "rocking back and forth on the bridge's railing." Quick as a flash, Dozier, a former college wrestler, made his move. Stepping onto the railing, he grabbed the man and threw him onto the pavement where the police subdued him.

That's not the end of the story. Dozier stayed in contact with Palmer. He kept sharing the gospel with him, led him to Christ, and now worships beside him at church. The city of Virginia Beach honored Dozier's heroic action with its Lifesaving Award. At the ceremony, Mayor Bobby Dyer said, "This is an individual who put his own life at risk to save another. [A]nd you know, that's a godly thing."[16]

When godly people walk through this world, there's a heavenly glow that lingers from their influence. God doesn't call all of us to tackle jumpers on bridges, but the world is full of hurting people who need saving—as only Christ can save them. In the process, they desperately need a person who loves and follows God to show up in their lives. They long for a glimpse of the glow of a godly person passing near them.

Why not let it be you? You have everything you need! So diligently add to your faith godliness.

> *Train yourself to be godly.*
> —1 TIMOTHY 4:7 NIV

Chapter 8

RADICAL KINDNESS

No one knows you like your mail carrier. Floyd Martin delivered mail on the same route for decades, serving five hundred people. Over the years he delivered mail, packages, good news, bad news, junk mail, large checks, gifts, and special deliveries to all the residents on his route in Marietta, Georgia.

But that's not all he delivered. He also delivered smiles, waves, encouraging words—and lollipops for the kids. He checked up on the neighbors and brought the newspapers to the doors of the elderly. He kept an eye open for anything that seemed amiss, and even fed treats to the neighborhood dogs and cats. When children on his route graduated from high school, he left twenty dollars in their mailbox. He wept when family members (or their pets) died and gave gentle hugs and kind words when he came across residents receiving bad news.

But it couldn't go on forever. Floyd finally announced he was retiring. The neighborhood was distraught to lose their postman, who'd become like their pastor. On his last day, a reporter for the *Atlanta Journal-Constitution* tagged along. At one house after another, people lined up to wish their mailman farewell. Some of the mailboxes were decorated with flowers, balloons, and signs. After Floyd delivered his last piece of mail, the neighborhood threw a block party for him, where everyone erupted in cheers and tears.

But the story has an incredible . . . well, postscript. As neighbors began sharing stories about Floyd on social media, someone mentioned that the postman once said he'd like to visit Hawaii. The tweets and posts went viral, and within a week over $32,000 came in from hundreds of people all over the country—from residents, former residents, families, and total strangers. Delta Airlines even stepped in and offered to provide the flights.

Floyd Martin's words to his "flock" were: "Thank you for caring about me. We've gone through good times and bad times together. . . . You were there when I needed you, even if you didn't know it. . . . I love you guys. I say that, I mean it. And that's what the world needs more of now—is love and caring and compassion and taking care of one another."[1]

Floyd Martin is right. His true story sums up exactly the kind of community and world we need right now.

My children—and maybe yours—grew up watching a Presbyterian minister named Fred Rogers whose television program was about such a community. *Mister Rogers' Neighborhood* gave children a model of what's been called "radical kindness." The show's producer, Margy Whitmer, said the success of the show was a bit of a mystery to everyone. "You take all the elements that make good television," she said, "you do the exact opposite, you have *Mister Rogers' Neighborhood*."[2]

That's just like brotherly kindness! You take everything discouraging you see around you every day—the drama, the arguing, the passions, the anger, the misunderstandings, the tension—and you do exactly the opposite. Wouldn't you want to live in a neighborhood like that?

Peter did. He believed the church should be that kind of neighborhood. Christian homes should be that way too. So Peter included brotherly kindness in his list of crucial qualities.

As we've learned, Peter opened his final letter by sharing that God has given us everything we need for a godly life through His precious promises—but we must put this gift to use. We have to diligently work on certain critical traits that define a truly Christlike life. So far we've looked at diligence, virtue, knowledge, self-control, perseverance, and godliness. Now we come to brotherly kindness. Peter said, "[Add] to godliness brotherly kindness" (2 Peter 1:7).

The word Peter used in his original language of Greek was *philadelphia*. I'm sure you recognize that word because it's the name of the city where America was born. William Penn, the founder of Pennsylvania, wanted to establish a city that was characterized by this biblical trait. To this day, Philadelphia's nickname is "City of Brotherly Love." Whether or not it lives up to that name is for others to decide. But Peter was telling us that as followers of Christ we should live up to that name. We must work hard to add to our godliness the quality of brotherly kindness.

Sometimes one biblical passage enlightens another. When I think of brotherly kindness, my mind goes to Ephesians 4:25–32, where the apostle Paul told us how we should treat our neighbors. Paul, too, felt the life of the church should have an atmosphere of brotherly kindness—of *philadelphia*. But what does that look like? Paul described it this way:

> Therefore, putting away lying, "Let each one of you speak truth with his neighbor," for we are members of one another. "Be angry, and do not sin": do not let the sun go down on your wrath, nor give place to the devil. Let him who stole steal no longer, but rather let him labor, working with his hands what is good, that he may have something to give

him who has need. Let no corrupt word proceed out of your mouth, but what is good for necessary edification, that it may impart grace to the hearers. And do not grieve the Holy Spirit of God, by whom you were sealed for the day of redemption. Let all bitterness, wrath, anger, clamor, and evil speaking be put away from you, with all malice. And be kind to one another, tenderhearted, forgiving one another, even as God in Christ forgave you.

This is an easy paragraph to study because it's essentially Paul's seven bullet points about brotherly kindness. Each is like a special delivery from the divine postal carrier to our hearts. The Bible tells us here to forge our friendships with trust, free our relationships from anger, feed those who are hungry, fortify others by our words, flush bitterness out of our spirit, find new ways of practicing kindness, and forgive others as Christ forgave us.

Can you imagine a better definition of brotherly kindness?

FORGE YOUR FRIENDSHIPS WITH TRUST

To build friendships with trust our lips must be kind, but also truthful and honest. Our words must be trustworthy and faithful. Put away lying, the Lord tells us, and speak the truth to our neighbors. Why? Because we are members of "one another" (Eph. 4:25).

Trust is essential to strong, healthy relationships. *Fixer Upper* stars Chip and Joanna Gaines recently celebrated their sixteenth wedding anniversary. Joanna wrote a note to their fans saying, "16 years and it feels like we're just getting started." Years ago, the two met at a Firestone store where Joanna was working. They hit it off immediately. Joanna said, "At first, I couldn't believe how kind Chip was—he had kind eyes and made me laugh a lot. I knew he was the one because I knew I could trust him."[3]

Do people know they can trust you? Brotherly kindness begins with a trustworthy spirit—with the willingness to be honest yet kind. Speaking honestly doesn't mean speaking bluntly or brutally. Stormie Omartian wrote, "I've known people who use the excuse of 'just being honest' to devastate others with their words. . . . [But] it's foolish to share every feeling and thought. Being honest doesn't mean you have to be completely frank in your every comment. That hurts people."[4]

It takes wisdom to know how to balance honesty and kindness. It also takes wisdom to know when and where to trust another person. Growing in brotherly kindness means growing in our ability to trust and be trusted.

Sometimes the Lord helps us know when we can even trust total strangers. In a busy city in Thailand, a man named Sorachat Sadudee picked up his eight-year-old daughter from school and got caught in heavy traffic. While they were stuck, the girl suffered an epileptic seizure, foaming at the mouth, jerking uncontrollably, and then passing out. Her father was frantic; there was no way to get out of the traffic jam. In a panic, he stuck his head out the window and yelled for help.

A young man named Itthiphon Petchphibunpong happened to be passing by on a motorcycle. He stopped to help when he heard the call. At first Itthiphon tried to clear a way through the traffic. When that failed, he offered to take the child to the hospital. Then the father did something remarkable. He decided to trust his daughter's life (and his own) to this unknown biker.

Sadudee gathered his daughter in his arms and got on the back of Itthiphon's motorcycle. The young man took off like a bullet, weaving through the traffic at lightning speed, racing to the hospital in four minutes. Sadudee held on to his daughter with a vice grip the entire time.

Itthiphon had a camera on his helmet, and when he posted the videotape online it captured the world's attention. It's more exciting than an action movie chase scene. You can't help but hold your breath until the biker pulled up to the emergency room where doctors were waiting to treat the girl.

"I couldn't thank him enough for his kindness," said the girl's father. "He saved my daughter's life. As soon as she is fully recovered, I'll take her to meet him and thank him again in person."[5]

I know we can't trust everyone in this world, but everyone should be able to trust *us*. Your spouse should be able to trust you; your neighbors too, and your coworkers. Even total strangers.

FREE YOUR RELATIONSHIPS FROM ANGER

As our attitude of brotherly kindness grows, it has a way of shoving aside the angry tempers that plague us. Ephesians 4:26–27 continues, "'Be angry, and do not sin': do not let the sun go down on your wrath, nor give place to the devil."

In this context, Paul wasn't talking about getting angry at things like traffic or the day's news. He was talking about getting mad at our "neighbor" (v. 25). When you're most tempted to lose your temper, it's often because of someone else, perhaps someone you love very much.

Interestingly, the Bible doesn't tell us never to be angry. Anger is a natural human response, but it must be governed. It's a dangerous emotion, as volatile as nitroglycerin, that must be controlled. That's why Paul quoted Psalm 4:4, which says, "Be angry, and do not sin."

In *Wishful Thinking*, Frederick Buechner wrote,

Of the Seven Deadly Sins, anger is possibly the most fun. To lick your wounds, to smack your lips over grievances long past, to roll over your tongue the prospect of bitter confrontations still to come, to savor to the last toothsome morsel both the pain you are given and the pain you are giving back—in many ways it is a feast fit for a king. The chief drawback is what you are wolfing down is yourself. The skeleton at the feast is you.[6]

Can you imagine a more destructive emotion than anger? Or one so universal? Like you, I sometimes battle discouragement, worry, and other emotions common to us all. But nothing can do more harm more quickly than anger. One moment of rage can wreck a multitude of lives. One rash word can ruin a friendship. One outburst can begin a life cycle of its own and create problems for decades to come.

Brotherly kindness is the biblical corrective for an angry spirit. Someone said, "The more you grow up, the less you blow up." Maturity involves learning to control how and when we express our anger—and how to replace it with brotherly kindness.

Steve and Annie Chapman have been ministering for Christ for years. They understand that whenever they speak or sing, they're in front of people who may have deep issues of anger in their hearts. Steve wrote of helping Annie with a women's event at a church. Everyone was pleasant and cordial, and the women were excited to be there. During her presentation, Annie explained she was working on a book about anger, and she asked the women if they'd fill out an anonymous questionnaire.

As Steve and Annie drove home to Tennessee after the event, Annie sifted through the responses. "Little did I know the levels of pain that had been inscribed on those pieces of paper," Steve wrote. "The ladies I had seen at that conference appeared so affable and good-natured on the outside. But after hearing Annie read with tears their anonymous cries regarding the anger that filled their souls, I wondered how so many of them could carry such pain in their hearts. It was an eye-opener for me."

Annie was not surprised. After years of working with women and studying the biblical resources about anger, she knew how many men and women carry a thick slice of anger inside them. Here are two of Annie's questions, with a few of the answers she received.

"When was the last time you were angry?"

- "Last night"
- "Yesterday"
- "Two days ago"
- "Every day"
- "Several weeks ago when my husband broke confidence again!"

"How did you express this anger?"

- "Threw something"
- "Cold shoulder"
- "By yelling and walking away"
- "Yelled at my three-year-old daughter"
- "Silent until I cried uncontrollably"[7]

How would you answer those questions?

We live in an angry world, and many of us are tired and under a lot of stress. We get angry and sin. But God doesn't want us to stay in such a condition. It's not His will for you to live with an angry spirit. You can see how that hinders brotherly kindness, can't you?

Growing in brotherly kindness means you're willing to develop the skill of Ephesians 4:26–27: "'Don't sin by letting anger control you.' Don't let the sun go down while you are still angry, for anger gives a foothold to the devil" (NLT).

If you're wondering how to start, I recommend a simple step: memorize Ephesians 4:26–27. Read it over and over out loud until you know it by heart; let it sink into your subconscious mind. The power of God's Word, when our brains are saturated with it, is incredible. It can overcome passions as strong as the anger that grips so many hearts today.

FEED SOMEONE WHO IS HUNGRY

Here's another secret to brotherly kindness: take care of someone in need. Ephesians 4 goes on to say: "Let him who stole steal no longer, but rather let him labor, working with his hands what is good, that he may have something to give him who has need" (v. 28).

Some of the Christians who first read this letter—the Ephesians—came to Christ from a background of thievery. They were shoplifters, cheaters, even burglars. Paul was saying that if they stopped stealing and instead worked hard with their hands to earn a livelihood, then they'll have something of their own to share with others. And that would give them the transformative experience of practicing brotherly kindness.

What a reversal! Instead of *stealing* from others, the former thieves were to *give* to others. Based on this verse, I advise you to work hard to earn a living and then use what you earn to care for those in need. The Bible says, "He who has pity on the poor lends to the Lord, and He will pay back what he has given" (Prov. 19:17).

Does someone in need come to your mind right now? Take a moment and think about it. Is anyone in your circle of contacts needing a little extra help? Brotherly kindness says, "I'm able to do a bit." When that kind of generosity becomes a constant lifestyle, you're starting to live in Ephesians 4.

Sometimes opportunities to help others arise unexpectedly. Officer James Riley of the Austin, Texas, police force was working the streets when he got a call that a little boy was wandering around a parking lot by himself. Riley found the boy and asked what he was doing. The boy said he was walking to a nearby store to get some snacks for his sibling and himself. Riley put the child in his police car and drove him home.

When Riley entered the house, his heart was moved with compassion because it was clear the family faced severe financial pressure. Riley got back in his cruiser, went to a nearby grocery store, and loaded up with snacks and easy-to-cook meals. The Austin Police Department then posted a picture of Riley's shopping cart on its Facebook page, generating thousands of responses and offers to help.[8]

It's as simple as that. The biblical concept of brotherly kindness is simply finding someone to feed, someone to help.

When Paul told us to give to "him who has need" in verse 28, he wasn't just speaking about literal food. He was talking about meeting the needs of others, whatever those needs may be. And sometimes the Lord leads us to go above and beyond a cart of groceries.

Little Gisele weighed only one pound, fourteen ounces when she was born, suffering from neonatal abstinence syndrome as a consequence of her mother's drug abuse. She spent almost three months in the NICU on ventilator support. Her parents were battling addictions and were unable to care for her. She was eventually transferred to Franciscan Children's hospital—tiny and alone, with no one to visit her.

But one nurse, Liz Smith, noticed her, felt incredible compassion for her, and began spending time with her regularly. "Since the moment I met her," said Liz, "there was something behind her striking blue eyes capturing my attention. I felt that I needed to love this child and keep her safe."

Liz became a foster mother to Gisele with a view toward reuniting her with her birth parents. When that plan fell through, Liz offered to adopt her. When Liz and her family and Gisele appeared before the judge to finalize the adoption, he stood up and said, "When a judge walks into the room, everyone stands out of respect. But today I stand in respect for you, Liz, because you deserve the respect from this room. A birthing day is a miracle. But adopting a child from miles away is destiny."[9]

In more ways than we can imagine, Liz is displaying the "brotherly kindness" that goes to great lengths to feed someone who is hungry.

You, too, can be a godsend to someone. The Lord has people for us to bless all along the way.

FORTIFY OTHERS WITH YOUR WORDS

That's not all. Your words need to enrich and uplift those who hear them. Paul continued in Ephesians 4:29: "Let no corrupt word proceed out of your mouth, but what is good for necessary edification, that it may impart grace to the hearers."

If you want an example of unwholesome talk, just turn on the TV or radio. Listen to the conversations around you. Even better, listen to your own words for a day and evaluate them through the grid of Ephesians 4:29.

The Bible is filled with verses about how we speak—the words we say and the tone we employ. But Ephesians 4:29 is among the most practical and helpful passages in Scripture when it comes to the subject of our tongues. Nothing we say should be unwholesome, which means unholy, unhealthy to others, destructive, or detrimental. Instead, our words should benefit others and build them up.

Many people are standing out in the rain of discouragement, as it were. Their hearts are soaked with heavy drops of disappointment and pessimism. But never underestimate the power of a kind word.

If you visit the National Gallery of Art in Washington, DC, look for the paintings of Benjamin West, one of America's great historical painters. When he was only six, Benjamin's older sister came to his home with her infant for a visit. While the baby took a nap, Mrs. West and the sister walked into the garden to gather flowers, asking Benjamin to watch the baby and use a fan to shoo away flies.

When the baby gently smiled in her sleep, the boy was enthralled. He reached for pen and paper and drew a sketch of the infant. As he was finishing, the two women returned and asked the boy what he was doing. Benjamin reluctantly showed them his drawing. "I declare he has made a likeness of little Sally," his mother said, and she bent over and kissed him. For the rest of his life and career, Benjamin West looked back at that moment—that kiss and kind word—as the birth of his career as an artist.[10] His mother's loving-kindness cemented confidence in his heart.

To practice brotherly kindness through your words, make a habit of complimenting at least one person every day. As you start your day in the morning, ask yourself, "Whom can I compliment today?" You'll be amazed at the gratitude that flows your way and fills your heart over time. People crave positive reinforcement. All of us do.

Abraham Lincoln wore a Brooks Brothers overcoat when he and his wife, Mary, attended a performance at Ford's Theatre on April 14, 1865. Shortly after 10:00 p.m., John Wilkes Booth crept behind him and fired a fatal shot into the president's head. Afterward, the personal belongings in his coat pockets were collected and given to his son, Robert Todd Lincoln, who put them in a box. They were later passed down to Robert's daughter, Mary, who donated them to the Library of Congress in 1937. The box was unopened until 1976.

Do you know what was in the box? What Lincoln had carried with him that fatal night in his Brooks Brothers coat? He had a couple of pairs of eyeglasses, a pocketknife, a gold watch fob, a white handkerchief, a cufflink, a Confederate five-dollar bill, a brown leather wallet, and several newspaper clippings. One of them extolled his accomplishments and began with the words: "Abe Lincoln is one of the greatest statesmen of all time."[11]

Though he was truly one of the greatest statesmen of all time, Abraham Lincoln endured unceasing criticism. He needed encouragement and affirmation as badly as his most beleaguered soldiers, and he was carrying an article that reassured him of his worth in his pocket when he died.

From the greatest to the smallest, we all crave words and actions that will encourage us, edify us, and build us up.

Imagine how Morey Belanger felt as she went to school on her first day of kindergarten. She was the first deaf student at Dayton Consolidated School, and it must have taken a lot of courage for her to walk through the door of her school. But the moment she crossed the threshold, what a surprise! Sign language posters lined the hallways. Teachers had begun learning sign language in their free time. And the entire elementary school had learned the alphabet and no less than twenty words in sign language to make Morey feel welcomed. The school even invited a princess—Cinderella—to come and sign with the children.[12]

That sounds like brotherly kindness to me! In every possible way, let your words and encouragement build up the hearts of others, and do so in Jesus' name.

FLUSH BITTERNESS OUT OF YOUR SPIRIT

Interestingly, Paul returned to the theme of anger in Ephesians 4:30–31. He wrote, "Do not grieve the Holy Spirit of God, by whom you were sealed for the day of redemption. Let all bitterness, wrath, anger, clamor, and evil speaking be put away from you, with all malice."

I've noticed something intriguing about this passage. In verses 26 and 27, Paul said that when we stay angry over a period of time, we "give a place to the devil." And in verse 30, he indicated that when we let bitterness grow in our hearts, we grieve the Holy Spirit of God.

A bitter spirit does two things at once: it grieves the Holy Spirit, and it delights the Devil.

To excel in brotherly kindness, you must work to resolve your deep personal issues. This is no easy task. But today there are many ways to seek help in freeing yourself from bitterness. With the guidance of the Holy Spirit, do what you need to do to release all bitterness, rage, and anger, along with every form of malice.

Many years ago, a student named Autherine Lucy Foster enrolled in the University of Alabama. In 1956, the school was an all-white institution, and Foster is African American. The hatred hit her like rolling waves, and she was expelled within three days after her presence brought protests and threats against her life.

In May 2019, sixty-three years later, Autherine returned to the University of Alabama to receive an honorary doctoral degree. She was eighty-nine years old, and this time her presence brought a standing ovation from the crowd. She told them, "I wasn't crying—tears were just rolling down my eyes because it's just so different."

Listen to this. Foster said, "The difference is that the crowds are here, but I see laughing faces instead of people frowning and displeased at me being here."[13]

There's a lot that concerns me about our society today, but when I hear stories like this one, it reminds me we've made some progress too. And what Foster modeled is symbolic of what Christ wants to do in our hearts. As we grow in Him, we can keep our hearts from bitterness even when we've been sinned against. The Bible says, "Those who look to him are radiant; their faces are never covered with shame" (Psalm 34:5 NIV).

FIND NEW WAYS TO PRACTICE KINDNESS

That leads us to Ephesians 4:32, which really brings the idea of brotherly kindness to fruition: "Be kind to one another, tenderhearted."

The theme of forgiveness pervades this passage, as we've seen, but so does the idea of kindness. That's the essence of *philadelphia*, and the good news is there are millions of ways, great and small, to put this into practice. Our opportunities to be kind are virtually infinite.

One day Ashley Jost of Columbia, Missouri, was shopping in a department store when she remembered she'd committed to a reading challenge with friends. Going over to the books and magazine section, she selected a book and took it home. She'd just started reading when a barking dog interrupted her. Throwing down the book, she went to check on the commotion. When she returned, a five-dollar bill lay on the floor. Where had it come from? She immediately went through her new book for clues. That's when she found a sticky note on one of the pages.

> To the person who buys this book: I am having a tough day. I thought maybe I could brighten someone else's with this little surprise. Go buy a coffee, donut, or a face mask. Practice some self-care today. Remember that you are loved. You are amazing. You are strong. Love, Lisa.

Ashley had no idea who Lisa was, but the note and five-dollar bill touched her deeply. She shared a picture of the note on social media, and thousands of people responded. Ashley's been inundated by people inspired to commit their own random acts of kindness, and she herself has passed along the blessing. Among her acts of kindness: leaving her own note and gift card inside a library book; giving a gift card to a friend going through a hard time; and paying for the coffee of the person behind her in the drive-through line.[14]

Kindness creates its own chain reaction, doesn't it? When you do something unexpectedly kind for someone else, the gesture takes on a life of its own. You never know where the ripple effects will end.

As I was writing *Everything You Need*, I read about eight hundred students from several Irish schools who lined up, formed a chain, and exchanged pats on the back to set a Guinness World Record. What if every reader of this book gave a pat on the back to someone today? We'd easily break that record![15]

There are many ways to give someone a pat on the back—even someone who's no longer around.

Clarence Hollowell of Jacksonville, Florida, only has one day off each week. Guess where he goes? To a local rundown cemetery where he cleans the tombstones of veterans. As an army veteran from a family of veterans, it bothered Clarence that some of the graves were becoming unreadable. With a plastic scraper, a soft-bristled brush, and a special cleaning fluid, he kneels beside each stone, cleans it, and writes down the names. Then he researches to find out something about the person. It's not a fast process to clean the stones. Each tombstone can take two or three weeks—and so far he's cleaned over six hundred.

Why?

"They were eighteen-, twenty-year-old boys that didn't come home," he told a reporter. They were standing by the headstone of James H. Savelle, who died in Fort Bliss, Texas, in 1918, from the influenza pandemic that followed World War I. "Everybody's gotta have a project, and I think if you can help the community, even better."[16]

FORGIVE OTHERS AS CHRIST FORGAVE YOU

Now we come to the seventh aspect of brotherly kindness: forgiveness. The Ephesians 4 passage ends, "Be kind to one another, tenderhearted, forgiving one another, even as God in Christ forgave you" (v. 32). Followers of Christ should be exceptional forgivers because we know how we have been forgiven.

Someone said, "Unforgiveness is like drinking poison, expecting it to kill the other person."[17]

To forgive someone is not to endorse or excuse their behavior. In his book about the power of forgiveness, Chris Brauns tells the story of Jennifer Thompson, a 4.0 student from North Carolina. One night in 1984, a man broke into her apartment, held a knife to her throat, and raped her. It might have killed her, but Jennifer was a determined woman. During the horrific ordeal she studied the man's face, looking for tattoos, scars, or anything that would identify him. Within days, she identified her assailant from a series of police photos, and she picked the man out of a lineup. Based on her testimony, Ronald Cotton was sentenced to life in prison.

Time passed. Jennifer got married and had triplets. One day a police detective and the district attorney knocked on Jennifer's door. They asked for a sample of DNA, which Jennifer provided. As unthinkable as it seemed, the DNA proved that another man, Bobby Poole, had actually been the rapist. Jennifer's testimony had sent an innocent man to prison.

For the next two years, Jennifer was haunted by the shame of her mistake. How could she have made such a terrible error? How could she have sent an innocent man to prison for ten years? One day, using all the courage she could muster, she got in her car and drove fifty miles to a church in the town where she'd been assaulted. There she met Ronald Cotton face-to-face.

"I'm sorry," she told him. "If I spent every day for the rest of my life telling you how sorry I am, it wouldn't come close to what I feel."

After a long pause, Ronald said, "I'm not mad at you. I've never been mad at you. I just want you to have a good life. We were both his victims."

The peace that came into their hearts could only come from the power of forgiveness. But that's not the whole story.

While in prison, Ronald Cotton and Bobby Poole had been in the same general area, and Ronald's hatred for Poole, whom he believed had committed the crime he'd been accused of, led him to make a blade out of a piece of metal to kill the rapist. Ronald's father pleaded with him to abandon his murderous plan and to turn his life over to Jesus. Battling great despair, Ronald Cotton finally took that life-changing step.

As Jesus came into his life, Ronald found that Christ had the power to bring peace to his heart. Ultimately, that's what gave him the remarkable ability to extend complete forgiveness to Jennifer Thompson.[18]

I know some of you reading these words have experienced terrible trauma in your life. Perhaps you've suffered at the hands of someone else, and you've never been able to make peace with what happened to you. I don't want to be simplistic; sometimes we need lots of time, counseling, and help. But I believe with all my heart that the basis of all emotional turnarounds is found in the grace of Jesus Christ and the power of the Holy Spirit. That's your foundation. When you personally experience His forgiveness, it changes you. It enables you to understand forgiveness, and it gives you the power to forgive others as God has forgiven you in Christ Jesus.

IMAGINE WHAT YOU CAN DO!

Let me end this chapter with another prison story—a much different story. Randy Geer was a corrections officer working in a maximum-security prison in Salem, Oregon. His father, Lt. Robert C. Geer, had also been a prison guard there—one of eleven corrections employees killed in the line of duty. He was slain in 1972, stabbed to death in the recreation yard.

Somehow, despite what happened to his father, Randy made up his mind to show compassion to the prisoners, and his career was marked with kindness. One prisoner said, "He never showed one ounce of retaliation. . . . He never used the tragedy of his family to make us feel any less of an individual. I was a convicted murderer. He didn't look at me as if I was one of them."

Randy Geer retired, suffering from diabetes. His condition worsened, and his left leg was amputated above the knee. As word spread, former and current inmates of the prison started reaching out to him. Those who could visit him did so, and many others wrote letters of encouragement. The prisoners he guarded became the support team who strengthened him.

Geer said, "I was so low in my spirits I was a bit worried about myself, about whether I could recover and wanted to recover." The visits and letters helped him turn the corner.

One inmate wrote, "Randy, you have always been such a compassionate being and a beacon to others. You've shown kindness to everyone and been a friend to so many."

Another wrote, "I'm sure it must be discouraging to face the fact that you've lost more mobility, but you haven't lost your capability or your importance in the world. I know this to be true because there are many of us who have found strength from your encouragement and just knowing you care."

When he was released from the hospital, his room at home was refurbished and readied for him by men he'd once guarded in maximum security.[19]

If a prison guard whose father was murdered on duty can become a walking legend of compassion behind the walls of a penitentiary, imagine what you and I can do every day in the freedom of our lives!

In a sense, we're all postal carriers assigned our individual routes on this planet. You're a special delivery messenger with a letter from heaven—the Bible—and with the words of the good news of Christ, postmarked with the blood of Calvary. Your zip code is wherever God sends you each day. By the time you finish your task, your message will touch thousands of people—maybe millions. Never let snow or rain or heat or gloom of night hinder you. Instead, be first class in your actions and attitudes. Seal your work with brotherly kindness, and God will stamp your life with His blessing.

> *Since God chose you to be the holy people he loves,*
> *you must clothe yourselves with tenderhearted mercy,*
> *kindness, humility, gentleness, and patience.*
> —COLOSSIANS 3:12 NLT

Chapter 9

SELFLESS LOVE

Tucked between massive buildings in the city of London is an unusual greenspace known as Postman's Park. A quiet spot for local workers to eat their lunches, the park has a circular walking trail, a small pool, and a fountain. It also has one of London's hidden gems: the Memorial to Heroic Self-Sacrifice.

The memorial is a simple wall of fifty-four ceramic plaques. Each plaque describes someone who selflessly gave their life.

ALICE AYRES
Daughter of a bricklayer's laborer who by intrepid conduct
saved three children from a burning house in Union
Street Borough at the cost of her own young life
April 24, 1885

DAVID SELVES, AGED 12
Off Woolwich
Supported his drowning playfellow and
sank with him clasped in his arms
September 12, 1886

MARY ROGERS
Stewardess of the Stella—March 30, 1899
Self-sacrificed by giving up her life belt and
voluntarily going down in the sinking ship

HENRY JAMES BRISTOW
Aged 8—at Walthamstow
On December 30, 1890—saved his little sister's
life by tearing off her flaming clothes but caught
fire himself and died of burns and shock

SOLOMON GALAMAN
Aged 11, died of injuries September 6, 1901
After saving his little brother from being run over in Commercial
Street. "Mother I saved him, but I could not save myself."[1]

Launched in 1900, fifty-three plaques were installed by 1931, and then the project was essentially forgotten. In 2007, a print technician named Leigh Pitt gave his life to save a nine-year-old boy from drowning. His colleagues, who knew about the memorial, asked if a plaque could be added in his name. The addition of his plaque was approved, and interest in the memorial was revived.[2]

Today, a nonprofit is trying to support and expand the project, because true heroism, love, and self-sacrifice are so desperately needed in our world. We long for examples of genuine love. Not the shallow emotions depicted in film and TV, but true, self-sacrificing love. Biblical love. God's love!

If I were building a memorial to honor self-sacrifice, I would put one large plaque in the middle bearing these words:

> God demonstrates His own love toward us, in that while we were still sinners, Christ died for us. (Rom. 5:8)

Through Jesus, God has given you the greatest love there is. In Romans 5:5, we read, "The love of God has been poured out in our hearts by the Holy Spirit who was given to us."

Everything in this book is summed up by that great biblical word *agape*—the heavenly brand of love that's ours in Jesus. *Agape* is self-sacrificing love, the kind of love that motivates people to give their all for God and others. In crises or heroic situations, our all may mean our lives. But in normal daily life, it means we will *live* for God and others, giving them our all with a selfless devotion and godly purpose.

That's where we've arrived in our study of 2 Peter 1:3–11. The apostle began, remember, by telling us we have the power to live a godly life. We don't need to despair over the difficulty of living in a godless age. The Lord has already given us His power, His promises, and His purpose.

Peter then insisted we do our part in developing a handful of critical life skills: diligence, virtue, knowledge, self-control, perseverance, godliness, and brotherly kindness. One by one, like dominos toppling each other, we've come closer to the final supreme quality of Christlikeness: love.

And here it is: add "to brotherly kindness love" (2 Peter 1:7).

Love is the final quality on Peter's list because it's the most important. It completes and gives meaning to the rest. Even if you cultivated all of the character qualities we've explored in this book and mastered them, they would be meaningless if they weren't saturated with love. Love is your deepest need and your highest blessing.

GOD LOVES YOU

Mike Yaconelli was traveling through San Francisco when he missed his flight home. Road-weary, angry, and homesick, he called his son, complaining. "Man, I'm stuck in the airport; it's been a horrible day. I've been traveling too much."

Instead of encouraging him, Yaconelli's son said, "You know, Dad, if you didn't travel so much, you wouldn't have things like this happen."

That didn't help, and Yaconelli just said, "Let me talk to my grandson." The boy was only two, but he got on the phone and started making two-year-old sounds. Yaconelli tried to make sense of the boy's words, but it's hard to communicate over the phone with a toddler. Then, as if by magic, he heard his grandson say in crystal clear words, "I love you, Grampa." Just like that, the sun came out and melted away his worry, frustration, and weariness.

Reflecting on the incident, Yaconelli said, "There are people who are so busy they're at their wits' end. If they'd only stop for a minute, they could hear the God of the universe whisper to them, 'I love you.'"[3]

God *does* love you. As I've said before, He always has, and He always will. The best way to understand how to add love to our brotherly kindness is examining how Jesus did it in John 13.

We often call 1 Corinthians 13 the "Love Chapter" of the Bible, but John 13 is the "Love Chapter" of Jesus. Here, Christ demonstrated His love in an astounding act of service and spoke His most powerful words on the subject.

The setting was the Upper Room on the last night before our Lord's crucifixion. It was the most poignant night in the life of the most powerful man who ever lived. All four gospel writers describe that night, but John takes us into its depths. Of the twenty-one chapters that comprise the gospel of John, six offer a record of this one evening. Every detail was burned into John's mind as if with a branding iron, and his account makes us feel as though we were there with him.

A love as dense as a London fog pervades this chapter. In every verse, you breathe it, smell it, see it, and feel it. So open the door with me, and let's enter this Upper Room.

The curtain of night has fallen over Jerusalem, and the streets are deserted. In every home, families are observing the Passover meal. The smell of roasted lamb wafts from every dwelling. The moon is full.

At one particular home, we walk up a set of stone steps to a large room. The meal is ready, and the twelve disciples are there. Oil lamps cast haunting shadows on the wall, and a feeling of foreboding hangs in the air. There has never been a night like this, and there never will be again.

During the meal Jesus breaks the bread and passes the cup and talks to His friends about His broken body and shed blood. The disciples are bewildered. That's where John takes up the story.

LOVE NAVIGATES OUR LIFELONG JOURNEY

John 13:1 says, "When Jesus knew that His hour had come that He should depart from this world to the Father, having loved His own who were in the world, He loved them to the end."

For three years, Jesus had led these twelve men throughout Galilee and Judea and through the truths of Scripture. He'd put up with their squabbling, their outbursts, and their mistakes. He'd nurtured their hearts and taught them the greatest truths the world has ever heard. Now it was time for Him to die, to rise again, and to ascend back to heaven. The same love that navigated His dealings with them for three years endured to the end. It never faltered. It never failed.

Jesus knows how to put up with your squabbling too, and with your outbursts and mistakes. His love is incredibly patient, always nudging you toward maturity. His love for you and through you enables you to navigate the twists and turns of life. As you grow in Jesus, His love helps you know how to act and what to say in every situation, to the very end. His love gives you the courage to serve Him all the way. God's love never falters. It never fails.

The nation of Burundi is one of the poorest countries in the world. Only three hundred doctors serve its eleven million citizens. One of those citizens is a pastor and evangelist named Michel Ntamubano, whose nine-year-old son, Amié, suffered a rare and terrible condition known as Blount's disease. The boy's legs were so badly bowed he couldn't walk, and no surgeons in the country could help him.

Amié's father brought him three hours over the mountains to Kibuye Hope Hospital, where Dr. Dan Galat, who was working with World Medical Mission, examined him. It was the worst case of Blount's disease he'd ever seen. Dr. Galat prayed, "God, unless you help me with this one, it won't be pretty."

As the day of the operation neared, members of Amié's church devoted themselves to prayer and fasting. "It was clear that this son was truly loved, and that God brought him to this small hospital for a purpose," Dr. Galat said. "I relaxed a little as I realized I had no choice but to somehow let God work through our feeble hands to be the answer to the faithful prayers of so many."

The surgery took several hours, and it was successful. Dr. Galat later explained the experience like this: "There are times in the operating room when we can sense the presence of God with us, and this was one of those times."[4]

If you're like me, you sometimes feel insufficient for the demands of life. Many days just feel hard. But that's when you lean on the love of Christ and pray, "God, my heart is open to You. Please help me with this problem."

As you grow in the love of Christ, you'll find yourself less anxious, even relaxed in the face of difficulty, because you've made the decision to let God work through your feeble hands and words. You've learned to sense the loving presence of God with you.

Think of it like this: What if Jesus' love had failed Him that night? Imagine the pressure He felt—twelve bickering disciples, one traitor, a fractured movement. Roman soldiers on their way. Trials and torture ahead. Execution. Goodbyes. The completion of His work. So much to say and so little time, and all these things were rushing together like meteors colliding. Had Jesus' infinite love faltered for even a flickering moment, everything would have turned out differently.

But He loved us to the very end, and His love guided Him through the terrible hours.

LOVE MOTIVATES US TO SERVE OTHERS

Ginger Sprouse went through a very messy and sinful patch in her life, but with the help of Jesus Christ she began rebuilding things. She may not have known the 2 Peter sequence we've been exploring in this book, but she followed it in practice. As she grew in her faith, she diligently wanted to develop a love that resembled Christ's. She prayed, "You have to show me how to be compassionate like Christ because I don't have it in me; it's not natural to me."

Near her home in Webster, Texas, a homeless man struggling with mental illness had stationed himself every day at a nearby intersection. That neighborhood near Houston's Johnson Space Center wasn't known for its homeless population, so Victor Hubbard stood out. Ginger learned he'd been standing there for three years, waiting for his mother to come back. She'd left him there when he was in his late twenties and never returned. Victor stood there day after day in the blistering sun or the pouring rain.

Ginger traveled that way often, and she began rolling down her window and talking to the man. They developed a friendship, and she started bringing him sandwiches and clothes. Sometimes she'd pull over for chats. Victor looked forward to seeing her car come into view.

One December when the weather became cold and dangerous, Ginger, along with her husband and two children, invited Victor to join them in their comfortable home. He moved in, and his new family began working with social services to get him help. Ginger and her husband own a cooking school, and they hired Victor. They took him to the optometrist to have his eyes checked. Other people who heard the story jumped on board, providing medical attention, clothing, a bicycle, and finances.

"She came around and she kind of saved me," Victor said. "It's like grace."[5]

Victor now lives next door to the Sprouses and is virtually part of their family. He loves his job in the food industry. Ginger and Victor have written a book, *Kinda Like Grace*, with all the proceeds going to help buy a house for someone else who may need the love of Christ and a roof over their head.

What motivated Ginger to roll down her window and chat with a stranger? It was the love of Jesus. It was Upper Room love.

Let's go back to that Upper Room. The story continues: "Jesus, knowing that the Father had given all things into His hands, and that He had come from God and was going to God, rose from supper and laid aside His garments, took a towel and girded Himself. After that, He poured water into a basin and began to wash the disciples' feet, and to wipe them with the towel with which He was girded" (John 13:3–5).

Jesus on His knees, clad in a towel, stripped like a servant! The very hands that would soon be pierced by nails tenderly rinsed the day's grime from twenty-four dirty feet. One by one, the flustered disciples felt the fingers of Jesus stroke their feet, wiping away the mud. He dried each foot carefully. He whose sandals they were not worthy to unlatch washed their feet.

The love of God exists in this world, and it's the only thing that really motivates genuine goodness on this planet. Not all of us are called to take in a homeless person, but when the love of Christ motivates you, you'll recognize the call.

In Cary, Illinois, there's a restaurant known for its homemade soup. Noah Dionesotes loves that soup and was a frequent customer at JC's Café, which is owned by chef Juan Carlos. One day Noah stopped coming. His multiple sclerosis was worse, and he was taking chemotherapy treatments. Stuck at home, he casually commented on Facebook that he missed JC's soup. Shortly afterward, there was a knock at the door. JC himself, Juan Carlos, had seen the post and was there with a pot of soup. It was hot, fresh—and free. He came the next day, and the next. For an entire year as of this writing, Juan Carlos has personally delivered free soup to Noah several times a week.[6]

The Bible says, "For Christ's love compels [motivates] us, because we are convinced that one died for all, and therefore all died. And he died for all, that those who live should no longer live for themselves but for him who died for them and was raised again" (2 Cor. 5:14–15 NIV).

When the love of Jesus lights a fuse of concern and benevolence in your heart, you can expect your actions to carry a powerful punch of gospel truth—God's Word in action!

LOVE IMITATES THE LORD JESUS CHRIST

Now let's take it a step further. When we learn to love as Jesus does, it's because we've decided to follow His example, to emulate Him. In the Upper Room Jesus went on to say, "If I then, your Lord and Teacher, have washed your feet, you also ought to wash one another's feet. For I have given you an example, that you should do as I have done to you" (John 13:14–15). Jesus taught His disciples a lesson twenty-four-feet long—literally.

Jon Bloom wrote, "If we love God most, we will love others best. I know this sounds like preposterous gobbledygook to an unbeliever. How can you love someone best by loving someone else most? But those who have encountered the living Christ understand what I mean."[7]

The key, of course, is understanding that *agape* love doesn't originate with us. We can't feel it, produce it, or experience it by ourselves. It flows from Jesus into our lives and then through us to others.

Amy Carmichael wrote,

I think of the love of God as a great river, pouring through us as the waters pour through our ravine at flood time. Nothing can keep this love from pouring through us, except of course our own blocking of the river. Do you sometimes feel that you have got to the end of your love for someone who refuses and repulses you? Such a thought is folly, for one cannot come to the end of what one has not got. We have no store of love at all. We are not jugs, we are riverbeds.[8]

Pastor Paco Amador serves a church in Chicago's Little Village, which is one of the largest Mexican communities in the Midwest, filled with young people, gangs, and violence. One afternoon Amador was asked to lead a prayer vigil for a young man gunned down by a rival gang. As he made his way to the house, large numbers of young people—gang members—converged around him, and his pulse raced. Then he realized they were simply heading to the vigil he was going to lead.

Intimidated by the circumstances, the pastor desperately wondered what to say and how to lead the service. Silently he prayed, *Jesus, what do You want me to do here?* Looking out over the crowd, his heart melted. Most of the scary-looking gang members were just kids, many of them teenagers. He was old enough to be their father. He decided to do his best to speak to them as he thought Jesus would.

He knew many of these youngsters had been abandoned or neglected by their fathers. So after introducing himself and the occasion, Amador took an unusual approach.

Today on behalf of your dads, I want to say to you what should have been said a long time ago. My son, my daughter, will you forgive me for not being there for you when you were little? Will you forgive me for not being there when you took your first steps, said your first words? Will you forgive me for not being there to throw the ball around when you were young? Will you forgive me for leaving you when you most needed me? Will you forgive me?

As the words poured from his lips, Amador began to weep. The tears flowed from his eyes. To his surprise, he saw tears filling the cheeks of those before him. "Something special happened at that moment," he later said. "A fearful pastor was becoming the conduit of heaven's tears. It was sacred. Jesus was there."

From that day, Pastor Amador had a special inroad to the young people in his community. They opened up to him, trusted him, and allowed him to become like a pastor to them. He said the great lesson was learning to pray in any given situation, "Jesus, what do you want me to do here?"[9]

Can you think of a setting in your life that would change were you to offer that prayer? Jesus returned to heaven at the end of His thirty-three years, but His Spirit has come into your heart. You represent Jesus wherever you are and wherever you go, which calls for His love, and for doing whatever He wants in any given situation.

Don't be intimidated by that. Be excited!

✗ LOVE ELEVATES THE EXPERIENCE OF LIFE

There's a special benefit that comes from growing in the love of Jesus, a true blessing. Jesus went on that night to say, "If you know these things, blessed are you if you do them" (John 13:17).

We might have expected Him to say, "If you know these things, others will be blessed when you do them." But Jesus specifically said, "Blessed are *you* if you do them."

Doing things for others keeps us from an unhealthy preoccupation with our own needs. In her book *Generous Love*, Becky Kopitzke tells the story of seven-year-old Mason, who battles muscular dystrophy. He's already endured several invasive surgeries, and each has been a dreaded event for him and his family.

Recently Mason underwent a major spinal procedure, and his mother, Keri, determined to prepare for it by helping someone else. It was her way of distracting her and her son from being preoccupied with apprehension. It was time to convert the energy of worry into a force for good works.

Keri's inspiration came from a wardrobe of outgrown shoes. Since Mason can't run, he doesn't wear out his shoes; he simply outgrows them. Keri decided she and her family could launch a campaign on behalf of Soles for Jesus, a ministry that delivers shoes to children in developing countries so they can attend school.

"We were in a perfect position to give up our gently used shoes to kids whose lives will be changed because of a simple pair of sneakers," Keri said, posting a Facebook announcement about it. The post was shared by friends and family, and soon neighbors, friends, coworkers, schoolmates, even strangers were rummaging their closets and rounding up their used shoes.

The day before Mason's surgery, Keri's family delivered more than two hundred pairs of shoes to Soles for Jesus—and they've continued collecting shoes ever since. "When you're going through something stressful, [you] forget that other people have their own problems," Keri said. "Our stress was not an excuse. We always say we're not going to be victims of this disease; we're going to live in victory. The shoe drive was one of the ways we could do that. It helped us all focus on how we're still in a position of blessing."

Although the shoe drive was about blessing others, Keri said she and her family were blessed more. "The whole experience really lifted our spirits and helped us to focus outward instead of inward on our pain and anxiety."[10]

You cannot share the love of Jesus without being blessed in the process. Every time the current of Jesus' love flows through you, you'll feel and experience the blessing of godly love. His love elevates the experience of life.

LOVE AUTHENTICATES OUR DISCIPLESHIP

And that brings us to the climax of our Lord's teachings on that evening. Jesus said, "A new commandment I give to you, that you love one another; as I have loved you, that you also love one another. By this all will know that you are My disciples, if you have love for one another" (John 13:34–35).

On the eve of His crucifixion, Jesus was reminding us of His love for us and His expectation that we take His love and give it to the world. Why? Because when the world sees how the brothers and sisters of Christ treat each other, it will prove and authenticate our message.

What was new about Jesus' command? It wasn't new in the sense that it never existed before. In fact, the Old Testament has two central love commandments:

- "You shall not take vengeance, nor bear any grudge against the children of your people, but you shall love your neighbor as yourself: I am the LORD" (Lev. 19:18).
- "You shall love the LORD your God with all your heart, with all your soul, and with all your strength" (Deut. 6:5).

The "new" element was the standard Jesus set regarding your love for others. "As I have loved you," Jesus said, "you also love one another."

This is the highest level of love in all the world. It's a love quite distinct from the Old Testament concept of loving one's neighbor as oneself. Jesus-love is this: love others, not as you love yourself, but as Jesus has loved you.

And how has Christ loved you?

Romans 5:8 says, "God demonstrates His own love toward us, in that while we were still sinners, Christ died for us."

John wrote, "By this we know love, because He laid down His life for us. And we also ought to lay down our lives for the brethren" (1 John 3:16).

That's a high standard, unreachable in your own power. But remember, God has given you everything you need to love in this way. Packed with His power and promises, you can learn to live your life for the good of others.

The love of Jesus attracts the world's admiration and respect. People may not like your message; they may despise your testimony; they may reject your biblical ethics. But they notice how you love, even in the smallest of ways.

Judy Douglass tells of boarding a crowded flight. The young woman who would be her seatmate had a heavy carry-on bag, and the man in front of her was in no mood to move his coat around in the overhead bin. He was quite rude to the young woman, saying her bag was too big and he'd claimed the space for his coat.

Judy spoke up, calmly but firmly reminding the man that the bin was shared space and his coat could go on top of the suitcase. He grumbled but moved his coat. Then Judy helped the girl with her suitcase. When they sat down, the young woman looked at Judy and said, "Why are you so different? Why did you do that for me?" That opened the door for Judy to share with her about the difference Jesus makes in our lives.

It's about as simple as that.[11]

God's love is to so dominate our lives that we are marked by it—to be recognized as different. Author John Piper said it like this:

> I personally like it when people put fish symbols on their cars and wear crosses and put "Hope in God" signs in house windows—but if you ask Jesus: what's the mark of a Christian that will set them off and help the world know that they are your disciples, his answer would be—his answer was—"By this all men will know that you are my disciples, if you have love for one another." Love for each other in the church is the badge of Christianity.[12]

 ## THE GREATEST OF THESE IS LOVE

Love is what matters most. The Bible says, "These three remain: faith, hope and love. But the greatest of these is love" (1 Cor. 13:13 NIV). So how can you diligently add to your faith love? Here are three everyday ways you can live out the world's most important virtue.

REMEMBER YOU'RE LOVED

John said, "We love because He first loved us" (1 John 4:19 NIV). In other words, loved people love. We can't love others like Jesus loves unless we are continually filled with His love.

Henry Drummond preached a classic message on love called "The Greatest Thing in the World." In one part of his message, Drummond was trying to demonstrate how the love Jesus has for us affects our love for others. Here is his illustration:

> If a piece of ordinary steel is attached to a magnet and left there, after a while the magnetism of the magnet passes into the steel so that it too becomes a magnet.[13]

The way we love others is by staying close to the love of Jesus so that His love becomes ours. Perhaps the best way to "magnetize" our hearts with Jesus' love is through prayer. Soak in His love for you by meditating on Scripture—particularly passages about God's love. Here are two Bible verses to turn into prayers.

- Ephesians 3:18–19 tell us to pray that we may grasp how wide and long and high and deep is the love of Christ and to know this love so that we may be filled to the measure with all the fullness of God.
- Philippians 1:9 is a prayer that our love will abound more and more in knowledge and depth of insight.

Take a moment and pray, "Oh Lord, help me better grasp how wide and long and high and deep is Your love, until I'm filled with the measure of Your fullness. May this love abound more and more in knowledge and depth of insight in me so I might better love others."

REIMAGINE YOUR RELATIONSHIPS

Steve Henning of Huntly, Illinois, was completely deaf as a result of contracting spinal meningitis when he was two years old. World War II was raging at the time, and doctors had a shortage of penicillin. That cost Steve his hearing. For the next fifty-seven years, Steve missed the sounds of music, of birds singing, of laughter, and of the voices of his loved ones.

In 2001, he learned about a surgical procedure that allowed sound waves to bypass the nonfunctioning parts of the ear and travel directly to the auditory nerve. He decided to undergo the procedure, but success was uncertain. For six weeks, they waited to activate the implanted device until the swelling in the ear decreased.

Finally, the day came to flip the switch and see if it worked. The audiologist programmed the cochlear implant and asked Steve's wife to say something. She leaned forward, looked at her husband, and gently said, "I love you."[14]

It worked! Those were the first syllables Steve had heard since age two. He broke into a smile and started his new life with the world's greatest three words.

Who in your life needs to hear those words? Call them on the phone or write them a letter or an email. Or even text them! Every morning ask the Lord who needs to hear they are loved and then tell them. You never know whose life you'll change by simply saying three small words.

Instead of asking what others have to offer you, reimagine your relationships as ways you can serve and encourage and bless others!

REORGANIZE YOUR PRIORITIES

Keeping our priorities straight and unchanged is a daily challenge. And the first step is knowing what goes at the top of the list. Once that's settled, other priorities fall in place more easily. As a follower of Christ, setting your top priority is clear: loving God and loving others.

Sometimes you don't love simply because it's not on your mind; it's not a priority. So how can you make love a priority in your life? Just like you make any other thing a priority—you schedule it.

Here's one way to do that. On your calendar or to-do list, write "John 13:34–35" next to all your assignments and meetings. Ask yourself, "How can I love like Jesus today?" After all, that's your most important job.

Police officer Aaron Franklin of Massillon, Ohio, had just started his morning shift when he got a call about juveniles trapped in water. He rushed to the scene, where a frantic teenager told him his friends had been swept into a culvert that carried water to the Tuscarawas River. Officer Franklin made his way down a slippery embankment, clung to a tree, and spotted two of the boys. With the help of other officers and firefighters, Franklin managed to rescue the two teenagers. Two more remained farther down the pipe, and they, too, were rescued. A fifth boy had traveled under the city, carried along by rushing water for half a mile. He was rescued as well.

With the boys safe, Franklin continued his patrol. His next emergency was a crash site where the vehicle was still in gear, with the driver slumped over the wheel. Franklin pulled the man from the car and laid him on the roadway, feeling for a pulse. The man was suffering a heroin overdose. After someone retrieved a Narcan kit from Franklin's car, he administered the prescribed dose and saved the man's life.

When local newspapers hailed Franklin as a hero for saving six lives in one shift, he was embarrassed. "Every day in this line of work you show up and you never know what's in store for you," he said. "Deep down, I hope, at least on that day, I did my job."[15]

Deep down, we know that our job as Christians is to go into every day ready to love, encourage, help, and save those who cross our paths.

We've been placed on earth to love as Jesus loved, and that's the crowning quality that completes Peter's list.

Crown all the qualities in life with the love of Jesus Christ. The world is thirsty for it. The people around you are starving for love—your family and friends, your neighbors and coworkers, your brothers and sisters. They all need someone to wash their feet, strengthen their courage, and give them a cup of cold water in Jesus' name. And when you find it difficult to follow in the steps of Jesus, remember this: it all starts with Jesus' love for you. He gave everything He had so you would have everything you need to love like He does!

Love is the last of the character qualities that Peter highlights. But he isn't finished with you yet; the best is still to come.

> *Beloved, if God so loved us, we also ought to love*
> *one another. . . . If we love one another, God abides*
> *in us, and His love has been perfected in us.*
> —1 JOHN 4:11–12

Chapter 10

THE BLESSING

One of the things my wife, Donna, and I have shared throughout our more than fifty years of marriage is our love of books. It's hard to remember a time when she hasn't been in the middle of a book. Unlike me, she reads them on Kindle. I'm still an old-fashioned hardback book reader. I like to write in the margins.

Several years ago on a coast-to-coast flight, Donna told me at the beginning of the flight what book she was reading, and within a very short time, she told me how the book ended. When I quizzed her about this, she explained that when she's having trouble following the book's plot, she reads the last chapter. Then she goes back and reads the rest of the book.

I teased her about this, and she replied, "Isn't that what you're doing when you teach from the book of Revelation? That's the final chapter on everything!"

She gave me that cute "gotcha" look of hers, and we laughed.

When I started writing this book, I was sorely tempted to follow Donna's example and teach the last chapter first, because this chapter explores some of the most motivating and uplifting verses in the Bible. In all my years of writing, I've never been more excited to write the final chapter! And no, it's not my relief at finishing. It's the glorious content Simon Peter gave me to work with.

We're about to dig into some of the richest verses in the Bible, verses that have lifted me up and kept me going during my most challenging times. I promise they'll do the same for you.

The apostle Peter wrote these words to you in his final letter. He wanted you to know that no matter how dark or dangerous the world may seem, God's power has given you everything you need for life and godliness. God isn't daunted by the signs or the times around you. His divine power is there to energize your life with a billion volts of grace. The Lord conveys this amazing power to you through His promises. Strengthened by those promises, you fulfill His purpose as you grow in eight essential qualities.

That's what we've studied thus far, but it's not the end of what Peter wanted to say to you. As you continue reading the last teachings of this imprisoned but impassioned apostle, he reveals a series of blessings waiting for you.

Peter's final gifts are blessings—seven marvelous blessings that roll into your life like ocean waves, dashing and glistening in the sunshine. I can't get them out of my mind; I hope I never do. Five are available now; two await you in the future. As you study them, they'll encourage you to put Peter's teachings into practice.

Here's this chapter in a nutshell: God has given you everything you need so He can bless you in every imaginable way!

For if these things are yours and abound, you will be neither barren nor unfruitful in the knowledge of our Lord Jesus Christ. For he who lacks these things is shortsighted, even to blindness, and has forgotten that he was cleansed from his old sins. Therefore, brethren, be even more diligent to make your call and election sure, for if you do these things you will never stumble; for so an entrance will be supplied to you abundantly into the everlasting kingdom of our Lord and Savior Jesus Christ. (2 Peter 1:8–11)

BLESSING ONE: GODLY MATURITY

The first blessing is the surge of godly maturity that accompanies your developing virtues.

After Peter listed his eight great qualities in verses 5–7, he wrote, "For if these things are yours *and abound*" (v. 8). Peter wanted early Christians to do more than have faith; he wanted them to devote themselves to growing deeper, wider, and richer in their faith. God wants the same for you—an abundant faith. Some of Peter's final recorded words were: "grow in the grace and knowledge of our Lord and Savior Jesus Christ" (2 Peter 3:18).

At times in Jesus' life, Peter seemed like the most immature disciple. But by the end of Peter's life, he had profound spiritual maturity and was ready to disclose the secret of how he acquired it—it was because of Jesus. It was Jesus and the process that was unleashed in Peter's life since their very first encounter. This is the process that's spelled out for us in 2 Peter 1.

The passage we're studying has only four sentences, and Peter used the words *these things* in three of them. *These things* refers to all the traits we've studied in this book—diligence, virtue, knowledge, self-control, perseverance, godliness, brotherly kindness, and love.

Peter said that all these can belong to you. They can abound in you. You can take possession of them, and they can take possession of you.

They can become integrated into your personality like veins of gold in granite. You, too, can have rock-like maturity.

God needs mature people in an immature world, for without them society would descend into chaos.

Speaking of mature people, meet Melvin Carter Jr., a retired police officer in St. Paul, Minnesota, and the father of the city's current mayor. He was an unlikely prospect for law enforcement. "I grew up ghetto and tough," he said. "I ran with the most notorious criminals in St. Paul. Before I became a cop, I was shot at by police. . . . My own story is a series of miracles. The elders [of my church] paved the way for me and held me accountable. By the love of my parents, my community and the grace of God, I was able to not just survive but thrive."

Carter spent twenty-eight successful years on the police force. Now he devotes his time to mentoring young men in trouble, working with them to develop maturity.

"Some of them I knew since they were born. Oftentimes it's circumstances. In so many lives, daddy's in prison, uncle's in prison, they're in poverty and moving four to seven times a year. These kids are stolen from community, stolen from their families. They need a vision beyond where they're at."

When Carter sits down with a troubled young man, he says, "You probably did something you're ashamed of which was either stupid or criminal or both. I come here to help you reclaim yourself. . . . I don't want to know what you did. There's more to you than that. You are our future. You are here for a precious purpose."

Carter understands the stirrings of maturity in young people. "Some kids are already past the point of no return," he said. "But, most times, something in their DNA knows they need to take some instruction from us. Even when they rebel or are dismissive, they really want it."[1]

Maturity comes with time and experience. As it develops, it gives you a vision that takes you beyond where you are today. You, too, are more than the sum of your mistakes, and somewhere in your soul you want someone to tell you how to grow up, how to become wiser, how to mature.

A word of caution: don't confuse maturity with perfection. Qualities that lead to maturity are ever-expanding and ever-increasing; you'll never perfect them while you live on this earth. No matter how much knowledge you have, there's always more to tap into. No matter how much perseverance you develop, you can become even more resilient.

At the end of each year, I take a spiritual inventory of my life. I look back over the last twelve months and honestly evaluate my walk with Christ. There are always areas where I could have done better. But I can also track spiritual growth in my life. That growth is related to the development of character and virtue—"these things" we've been studying. When I see that growth in my life, my confidence as a Christian is strengthened. I am Christ's, and He is mine. I am spiritually alive and am becoming spiritually mature.

How are you doing in the maturity department? How mature is your faith, your joy, your patience, your wisdom in handling difficulties, your instincts for making wise decisions? What about your godliness, friendliness, and brotherly kindness? Don't be discouraged. Be diligent! Let these qualities abound in you. In the process, maturity happens.

BLESSING TWO: GROWING PRODUCTIVITY

Second Peter 1:8 goes on to say, "For if you possess these qualities in increasing measure, they will keep you from being ineffective and unproductive" (NIV). Peter put that in the negative, but let's restate it like this: "If you possess these eight qualities and grow in them, you'll be increasingly effective and productive in whatever you do for Christ."

I read about a woman who works with her sisters in event planning.

They do everything from wedding receptions to birthday parties. Over the years they've accumulated a garage full of decorations. A couple of years ago, the Lord prompted this woman to volunteer at her church, and soon she was decorating the building for every season and event.

"I take such joy in this because most of the people in our church are poverty stricken and live in Section 8 housing which is often rundown," she said. "It's been amazing to see the response people have had to what I would consider simple decorations we put throughout our church. They feel like it's been spruced up just for them. . . . It brings me so much joy to see the smiles on their faces. . . . since they probably face more hardship in one day than I do in a month."[2]

Each of us has special gifts, talents, passions, opportunities, and assets for God's kingdom. Are you using your gifts effectively? Is God using you? I know of a man who used to pray, "Lord, use me!" Then it dawned on him to change his prayer to, "Lord, make me useable!"

That's what the virtues in 2 Peter do—they shape us into fruitful and effective servants for the kingdom. The key to productivity in Christian ministry is the diligent development of godly character in your life. As God works *in* you, developing you into a mature believer, He'll then work *through* you so you can be a blessing to others.

Rodney Smith Jr. came from Bermuda to Alabama for schooling but was having a hard time deciding what to do with his life. "I prayed that God would use me as His vessel," he said. One day he was driving down the street and saw an elderly man struggling to cut his grass. Rodney stopped and helped him finish the job.

"When I was driving away, I was amazed at how good that felt. And I truly believed God was speaking to me. So as I was finishing up my computer science degree, I would find widows, veterans, disabled or elderly people that needed their grass cut and just do it. For free.

I couldn't believe how it touched them. So many of these people had lost a lot of joy in their lives. More than cutting their lawn, I'd spend time listening to their stories. So this was not just about taking care of their yard; it was showing them they matter and that God cares for them."

Rodney started recruiting kids from the city and encouraging them to take care of yards, raking leaves in the fall and shoveling snow in the winter. He gave T-shirts to any young person who took care of ten lawns. If they did fifty lawns, he gave them a free lawn mower. Rodney's unique ministry provides lawn care and loving fellowship to single moms, elderly people, disabled vets, and many others. It also takes young men off the street, mentors and trains them, and teaches them the power of giving themselves to a cause.

Today his ministry—Raising Men Lawn Care Service—has nearly three hundred young boys and girls working throughout the United States. Rodney travels all over America cutting lawns and giving talks about how God can use us to serve others.[3]

Rodney's story illustrates this principle: spiritual growth is the father of spiritual productivity. That's what Peter promised. The New Living Translation of 2 Peter 1:8 puts this principle in plain and simple language: "The more you grow like this, the more productive and useful you will be."

If there are ten thousand maturing Christians in your city, there will be ten thousand maturing ministries for God's glory, each unique. If there are five hundred maturing believers in your town, that's how many personal ministries will develop. Each of us will be productive and fruitful as we develop the qualities Peter described. We can't help it.

And no matter how long you live, you never outgrow this principle: "They shall still bear fruit in old age; they shall be fresh and flourishing" (Ps. 92:14).

BLESSING THREE: GREATER CLARITY

The third blessing that comes with the development of these eight virtues is greater clarity. Second Peter 1:9 says, "For he who lacks these things is shortsighted, even to blindness."

Shortsighted people have trouble seeing how to live, how to speak, how to act, what values to hold, and what opinions to express. They're blinded by immaturity and by the Devil. They're blind to the spiritual truths needed to function properly in this present world.

Have you ever been fitted for glasses? The last time I visited the optometrist, I sat down in a chair in a darkened room, and he pulled around a large device that looked like a complicated set of interlocking binoculars. Placing my chin on the pad, I looked through the lens. Everything was blurred. As he turned a wheel, I heard a click. "Is that better or worse?" he asked. Click by click, things became clearer until I could read every letter. Based on that gradual process, he knew my prescription.

The eight qualities Peter listed are like those lenses. Click by click, the Great Optometrist clarifies your vision as you mature in His prescribed qualities. Bit by bit, you're better able to read the handwriting of His will. You're able to trace the letters of His grace. You're able to discern the times and know how to act. You're able to interpret the details and see things in their context—in the context of His Word and His providence.

Lately, I've fallen in love with the word *clarity*. It means seeing things as they are, not simply as we wish them to be. It also means seeing things by faith and understanding that God is working things for our good. This is a constant drumbeat in the Bible. Take the Psalms, for example. The writer of Psalm 119 said, "Open my eyes, that I may see wondrous things from Your law. . . . Turn away my eyes from looking at worthless things, and revive me in Your way" (vv. 18, 37). As our eyes are opened to God's working through all the details of life, we're like the psalmist, who said, "This was the LORD's doing; it is marvelous in our eyes" (Ps. 118:23).

The return of Christ comes into increasingly sharper focus as we grow in Him. Peter's short letter is filled with information about the Lord's Second Coming. The subject occupies most of the last chapter. One of my former professors at Dallas Seminary, Dr. Zane Hodges, made this observation: "Since, in this small epistle, the apostle Peter lays heavy stress on the reality and certainty of the Lord's coming . . . the apostle is probably thinking of believers who no longer look ahead to the Rapture. Instead their vision is severely limited to the here and now. People who live simply for the present time, or for the present world, are tragically 'short-sighted.'"[4]

Three times in 2 Peter 3:11–14, we're told to look forward to the Lord's return.

> Therefore, since all these things will be dissolved, what manner of persons ought you to be in holy conduct and godliness, *looking for* and hastening the coming of the day of God, because of which the heavens will be dissolved, being on fire, and the elements will melt with fervent heat? Nevertheless we, according to His promise, *look for* new heavens and a new earth in which righteousness dwells. Therefore, beloved, *looking forward* to these things, be diligent to be found by Him in peace, without spot and blameless.

That's anticipation! That's clarity—about the present and about the future. What a blessing!

When Ronald Reagan was a child, he was badly nearsighted, but he didn't know it. Neither did anyone else. He saw much of the world as a blur. One day when he was thirteen or fourteen years old, his father took the family for a Sunday drive through the green countryside around Dixon, Illinois. Reagan was sitting in the back seat and noticed his mother, Nelle, had left her eyeglasses on the seat. Picking them up, he put them on.

"The next instant, I let out a yelp that almost caused [my father] to run off the road," Reagan wrote. "Nobody knew what I was yelling about, but I'd discovered a world I didn't know existed before. Until then, a tree beside the road looked like a green blob and a billboard was a fuzzy haze. Suddenly I was able to see branches on trees and leaves on the branches. There were words as well as pictures on billboards. 'Look!' I shouted, pointing to a herd of grazing dairy cows I hadn't seen before. I was astounded. By picking up my mother's glasses, I had discovered that I was extremely nearsighted. A new world suddenly opened up to me."[5]

As you grow in the grace of Jesus, your vision becomes increasingly clear. You see His blessings more quickly. You learn to focus your vision on things unseen, for the things that are seen are temporary, but the things that are unseen are eternal (2 Cor. 4:18).

BLESSING FOUR: GRATEFUL MEMORY

The next blessing that comes from abounding in the character traits God desires is a grateful memory. And once again, Peter used the negative to drive home the positive: "He who lacks these things is shortsighted, even to blindness, and has forgotten that he was cleansed from his old sins" (2 Peter 1:9).

Allow me to restate: If you grow in the qualities we've studied, you'll never forget how Christ has forgiven you of past sins. You'll keep Calvary in mind, always remembering how Jesus rescued, restored, and blessed you.

Peter warned against a complacent, satisfied faith. Instead, he wanted you to keep fresh in your memory the joy and thrill of your salvation. When you diligently seek to grow in Christlike character, you'll never lose the delight of what's happened to you.

As a young man, John Newton, who wrote the hymn "Amazing Grace," was involved in the evils of the slave trade. God saved him through the power of the blood of Christ, and Newton eventually became one of the greatest preachers and pastors of his age. He joined forces with England's abolitionists and saw the slave trade banned from the British Empire in 1807.

Near the end of his life, Newton received a visit from a friend, William Jay, who later wrote, "I saw Mr. Newton near the closing scene. He was hardly able to talk; and all I find I had noted down upon my leaving him was this: 'My memory is nearly gone, but I remember two things: That I am a great sinner and that Christ is a great Savior.'"[6]

Something I've noticed through years of reading the New Testament is the way the apostle Paul kept cycling back to the moment of his conversion on the Damascus Road. He never forgot what God did for him that day. He never got over it.

You can get over a lot of things. You can get over loss and sadness and the problems that come with life, but you never want to get over Jesus or what He has done for you. As you grow in Him, your gratitude increases.

The best way to cultivate a grateful memory is to prompt yourself to be thankful. Always make it a point to say, "Thank You, Lord" throughout the day as He blesses you. Without His grace, your memory would be marred by regret, remorse, and shame. But through the blood of Christ, God has thrown all that behind His back. He's cast it as far as the east from the west. We should never look back in anguish or embarrassment at anything in our lives, for God has washed away our sins. As we grow in Him, we grow in gratitude.

Let God heal your bad memories by enhancing your grateful recollections of His grace, and learn to be thankful to Him every day. He met you on your own Damascus Road; He's washed away your guilt; He's cast your shame behind His back; and He has given you a legacy of grace. Make sure you never get over it.

BLESSING FIVE: GENUINE STABILITY

Here's something else you'll discover as you cultivate the traits of godliness: these traits bring genuine stability into your life. Peter said in the next verse, "Therefore, brethren, be even more diligent to make your call and election sure" (2 Peter 1:10).

What does it mean to "make your call and election sure"? J. B. Phillips, in his version of the New Testament, put it this way: "Set your minds, then, on endorsing by your conduct the fact that God has called and chosen you." Peter was not saying you can work your way to heaven. He was concerned about those who profess Christ outwardly but whose testimony isn't confirmed by the way they live.

In Peter's day, as in ours, many false teachers made great statements about their supposed godliness while they lived very ungodly lives. Peter devoted the entire second chapter of his letter to these people, calling them "wells without water, clouds carried by a tempest" (2:17). Genuine believers, on the other hand, exhibit their salvation by their growth in godliness and the stability it brings them.

As you grow in Christ, you'll become more emotionally stable, more spiritually sturdy, and more solid in your beliefs, your behaviors, and your relationships.

John MacArthur wrote, "An alarming number of Christians seem to lack spiritual stability. Many are 'tossed to and fro' by the waves and carried about by every wind of doctrine, by human cunning, by craftiness in deceitful schemes. . . . Others lack moral purity. Many are driven by their emotions rather than sound thinking. While we still proclaim a sovereign, all-powerful God, our conduct often belies our creed."[7]

That's exactly what Peter was getting at. When you grow in the traits of godliness, your conduct begins matching your creed, or your beliefs. You confirm your faith by your faithfulness, and it brings stability to your life.

This was on Gretchen Saffles's mind as she faced a major relocation. Her husband was offered an exciting new job, but it meant packing up their belongings and moving with their little boy to a distant community. One day as Gretchen sat looking at the boxes in their near-empty house, she felt as if chaos and disorder had descended on her. But she stopped to consider something.

"As [we] began walking through this very brief and intense season of transition, the Lord has been opening my eyes to several aspects of His character; specifically, His stability when our world is unstable."

"I'm a creature of comfort," she wrote. "I thrive in a clean, put together home. I sleep better at night when the kitchen counters are wiped down and the laundry is folded." But, she said, when the world is "unstable, chaotic, and 'out of our control,' we can trust in God's steady, consistent, never-ending grace. He is our stability during times of transition. . . . Because ultimately, if the entire world crumbled in an instant, His Word would still stand."[8]

Wow! That's a great way of saying it. Even if the entire world crumbles in a cloud of dust, God's Word will stand. Nothing can shake the Lord, for He is unshakable. Nothing can destabilize Him, for He is unchanging. Nothing can surprise Him, for He is omniscient. Nothing can worry Him, for He is Lord of all. As you grow in godliness—as you become more and more like Him—you'll experience genuine stability of heart, mind, and soul.

BLESSING SIX: GUARANTEED SECURITY

That brings us to the sixth blessing: guaranteed security. Notice how emphatically Peter put it in 2 Peter 1:10: "For if you do these things you will never stumble." Remember, "these things" are the eight character qualities we've studied. Could Peter have been more emphatic in his statement? If you keep growing in these traits, you'll *never* stumble.

In other words, you'll never stumble on the highway to God's eternal home. You'll never tumble off the edge of the cliff and be lost. Peter didn't mean you'll never make a mistake or commit a sin. He meant you never have to worry about whether you're going to heaven. Your progress in the faith will serve as reassurance of your salvation.

J. D. Greear wrote that by age eighteen he'd probably asked Jesus into his heart five thousand times. One Saturday morning when he was four or five, he approached his parents asking about heaven. They explained the gospel message to him, and he asked Jesus to come into his life. His parents and his pastor felt it was a sincere decision, and they wrote the date in his Bible. "I lived in peace about the matter for nearly a decade," he said.

But in ninth grade he heard his Sunday School teacher say that many who think they're saved will awaken on the Judgment Day to hear Jesus say He never knew them. "I was terrified," wrote Greear. "Would I be one of those ones turned away?"

He asked Jesus to come into his heart again, this time with a resolve to be much more intentional about his faith. He was baptized again; but again, new doubts arose. He prayed the sinner's prayer again and again. "I walked a lot of aisles during those days," he wrote. "I think I've been saved at least once in every denomination."

In all, Greear was baptized four times! "Honestly, it got pretty embarrassing. I became a staple at our church's baptism services. I got my own locker in the baptismal changing area."[9]

But here's the point: as Greear began growing in Christ and in the traits of godliness, his doubts and fears melted into faith and confidence. His growing maturity and stability led to growing confidence and security. Today he'll be glad to tell you how he knows without doubt that he's heaven bound.

If you have truly repented of your sins and trusted in the death and resurrection of Jesus Christ for salvation, you are saved! And as you grow in Jesus Christ, you will *know* you are saved. The very growth you experience in Christ will provide reassurance you've been born again. Similarly, as you grow in the eight qualities Peter described, you won't stumble into doubting your salvation because you'll be drawing from His divine power and standing on His precious promises. His very personality will surge through you to create the qualities that give stability and security to life.

BLESSING SEVEN: GLORIOUS ETERNITY

That leads us to the seventh blessing—a glorious eternity! Follow Peter's logic in 2 Peter 1:10–11 as he brought the paragraph to a thrilling climax: "Therefore, brethren, be even more diligent to make your call and election sure, for if you do these things you will never stumble; for so an entrance will be supplied to you abundantly into the everlasting kingdom of our Lord and Savior Jesus Christ."

Peter isn't suggesting we get into the Lord's kingdom by building character in our lives. We can't work our way into heaven on our own merits or by our own efforts. Instead, he's saying that if we diligently add these spiritual qualities to our Christian lives, we'll be given a rich or an abundant entrance into eternity.

One writer said, "Believers in Christ are secure forever, whether they add Christian character qualities to their faith or not. What is at stake here . . . is not kingdom entrance, but *abundant* kingdom entrance."[10]

In my book *Living with Confidence in a Chaotic World*, I compared heaven to a safe and pleasant harbor. Throughout our lives, we sail godward toward that harbor, moving through the storms and the rocks that lurk in the waves. Some ships barely make it into port. The crew is exhausted and near mutiny, the sails are torn, supplies are low, and the ship has sprung many leaks. It's not exactly a hail-the-conquering-hero kind of arrival.

But we don't have to float into harbor with our sails down and our spirits defeated. Peter was telling us that diligent believers are like attentive captains and sailors; they sail with discipline, manning the watchtower, maintaining the ship, keeping morale high among the crew. Storms will come, but God has given us what we need to come through each one stronger.[11]

LIFE BELOW THE WATERLINE

More than twenty years ago, I was stricken with stage four lymphoma cancer. When I was first diagnosed, I went to the Mayo Clinic in Rochester, Minnesota, where I underwent major surgery. I will never forget those days in Rochester, and especially my initial moments when I returned to my home in San Diego.

As soon as we arrived, I found my way to my favorite recliner in our living room. Within a few minutes, Donna brought me a stack of letters and get-well cards that had arrived while we were away. On top of the pile was a book sent to me by the publisher.

Before I tell you about that book, I want to tell you what was going through my mind that day as I returned home. I was asking God a lot of questions. I'd gotten past the "why" question and was concentrating on the "what" questions. Like: *What am I supposed to learn from this frightening experience? What lies ahead? What do You want me to do going forward? What does all this mean?*

The book on top of the pile of cards had this intriguing title: *The Life God Blesses*. It was written by Gordon MacDonald, a man I'd met and admired. As I read that book, I couldn't help but think that God, not the publisher, sent it to me through the mail. It was just the right message, and I was in just the right place to read it prayerfully and carefully.

In the front of that book was a story I've never forgotten. More than any story I've ever read, it illustrates the message I've tried to convey to you in the pages of this book.

The story involved an American yachtsman named Michael Plant, forty-one, an experienced sailor with more than 100,000 miles at sea. Plant started sailing at age nine, and he held the record for the fastest solo circumnavigation by an American. On October 16, 1992, Plant sailed out of New York Harbor bound for France. His sixty-foot sailboat, the *Coyote*, was top of the line. Its design, hull, materials, fabrication, equipment, and comfort were unparalleled.

But something went terribly wrong. Within two weeks, Plant was missing and his radio frequencies went silent. Authorities began searching the vast North Atlantic. Airline pilots listened for emergency signals. Ships in the area kept a constant lookout. Plant's friends felt growing apprehension.

Finally, the *Coyote* was spotted, floating upside down 450 miles northwest of the Azores Islands.

Plant's fellow sailors were mystified. Sailboats normally don't capsize because they're designed with a ballast beneath the waterline, a weight bolted to the bottom of the ship to keep it upright. They're built to take a pounding and then, like a child's punching balloon, right themselves after every blow. The *Coyote* was designed with a ballast of 8,400 pounds—but the ballast was missing.

What happened to it is a mystery to this day. Some sailors believe it was sheared off by debris in the sea or even by a passing whale. But the boat's hull showed no signs of that kind of damage. Others speculate it wasn't bolted on strongly enough. Most experts believe the ballast was damaged while Plant was preparing for his journey, when the boat became mired in the mud and had to be dragged out. These experts think the ballast was weakened at that point and then later was dislodged by winds, storms, and currents.

Whatever the reason, without the ballast to hold it steady through troubled waters, the boat capsized, and Plant's body was never found.

The lesson is clear: The life of godliness is not built out in the open; it's nurtured trait by trait, gift by gift, just as Peter explained in his final, beautiful letter to you.

There are storms ahead for all of us. If you ignore the quiet but essential traits outlined in this book, you're headed for troubled waters without the ballast of God's gifts to stabilize you. The qualities you need to get through those storms and get to heaven triumphantly are available to you in abundance. God has indeed given you everything you need.

The only question is: What are you going to do with these precious character qualities of diligence, virtue, knowledge, self-control, perseverance, godliness, brotherly kindness, and love?

My friend, there needs to be more to you than meets the eye. Down below the waterline, deep in your heart, I urge you to carry the ballast of God's power, His promises, and His purposes. This is the gravity of His grace that keeps you steady in the storm. May God bless and keep you in His promises forever.

To Him be the glory both now and forever. Amen.

—2 *Peter* 3:18

EPILOGUE

Can you conceive of 860,300,000 words? That's how many words the average person speaks in a lifetime.[1] Some people are quieter, of course, while those who are more talkative can speak more than a billion words. I may be one of them—I'm a preacher!

Now, imagine you've spoken 860,299,000 words and you only have enough time for your last thousand. You know the end of your life is very near, and every remaining phrase is precious. What would you want recorded for posterity?

Simon Peter's last message, the book of 2 Peter, is just over a thousand words in length. That's shorter than this epilogue. I can envision him in the candlelight of his Roman cell, scratching out his final letter—the only way left for him to speak to the world. He weighed every word, considered every thought, and prayed over every sentence. No wonder this book is so rich!

Everything You Need is based on one amazing paragraph from this letter: 2 Peter 1:3–11. Now I'm down to my own last words as it relates to our study together. So let me close by focusing on a single term we sidestepped earlier: *faith*. I was saving it for just now.

Here's where we find it: "But also for this very reason, giving all diligence, add to your *faith* virtue, to virtue knowledge, to knowledge self-control, to self-control perseverance, to perseverance godliness, to godliness brotherly kindness, and to brotherly kindness love" (2 Peter 1:5–7).

Notice that faith is the foundation for everything else. Faith comes first. Apart from Christ, you have no divine power. Without Him, you have no precious promises. And you'll never develop the essential qualities of virtue, knowledge, self-control, and the rest. Without faith, it is impossible to please God.

Peter used the word *faith* twice in 2 Peter. The first time came in the first verse of his epistle: "Simon Peter, a bondservant and apostle of Jesus Christ, to those who have obtained *like precious faith with us*" (1:1).

Peter had an incredible history with the Lord Jesus. It began one day as he and his brother, Andrew, were casting their nets into the Sea of Galilee. The Teacher from Nazareth passed by. He said to them, "Follow Me, and I will make you fishers of men" (Matt. 4:19). Those words triggered something powerful within Peter, and he immediately left his nets and followed Jesus. The next three years of his life were extraordinary. No one ever saw such things as Peter and his companions witnessed.

Peter watched Jesus cast an impure spirit out of a man in Capernaum. He listened as Jesus preached to the vast crowds that gathered in the Galilean meadows. Jesus moved into Peter's house and lived with his family. When Peter's mother-in-law was burning up with a fever, Jesus took her by the hand, and she was suddenly as healthy as ever. She got up and began serving them all.

For three years Peter lived alongside Jesus, traveled with Him, talked to Him, studied Him, and sometimes argued with Him. There was a special bond between the two. When the disciples were caught in a storm, Jesus walked across the tempestuous lake to get to them, and Peter impulsively tried to walk on the water too. He made it a few steps before losing his nerve and sinking. The Carpenter's hand caught him, pulled him to safety, and waved away the storm.

When Jesus asked His disciples, "Who do you think I am?" Peter was the one who replied, "You are the Messiah." When Jesus was transfigured, it was Peter who blurted out how glad he was to be there with Moses and Elijah.

Peter traveled to Jerusalem with Jesus on that final, fateful journey, and he was part of the celebration on Palm Sunday as the people cried "Hosanna!" He was in the Upper Room when Jesus broke the bread and passed the cup and washed the disciples' feet.

In the Garden of Gethsemane, Peter drew his sword to defend Jesus against the arresting soldiers, but he again lost his nerve and sank. In the darkest moment of his life, he denied knowing Jesus and watched the Savior's crucifixion from afar. But after the resurrection, Jesus met with Peter and loved him; and three times Peter responded, saying, in effect, "I love You too."

Peter was there when Jesus ascended into the sky and returned to heaven. It was Peter who led the early church. When the Holy Spirit came crashing like a ball of fire into the Upper Room on the day of Pentecost, Peter preached a great sermon resulting in more than three thousand conversions. From that point, Peter was a man on fire, and under his powerful preaching the church spread around the world.

Now, as he sat to finish the letter we've been studying, he was within days of his execution, but he remained undaunted. At the end of his letter and his life, with eagerness and optimism, he wrote that he looked forward to a new heaven and a new earth, where righteousness dwells.

What a powerful story! What a precious faith!

Yet Peter's faith was no more precious than yours can be. Let me paraphrase his words: "I've had quite an experience with Jesus Christ during my life, but I want you to know you can have an experience with

Him that's just as personal, just as powerful, and just as precious as mine. My story is unique to me, and your story is unique to you. You can be just as close to Christ, just as strong in Christ, and just as useful to Christ as I've ever been."

I want to do all I can to make sure you have a faith as precious as Peter's. My final message to you is this: follow Jesus. Become His disciple. Repent of your sins, turn from your faults and failures, and let Jesus begin to make you a fisher of men and women. Let Him begin to make you into the *petros*—the rock of strength—He wants you to be.

Adrián Ferrari reminds me a lot of Peter. He was born in Buenos Aires, Argentina, in a home that was destroyed by delinquency and drugs. His life spun out of control, and he contracted AIDS through drug abuse and illicit activities. He was arrested, and while in jail, he learned his brother had been killed in an act of violence.

Adrián obtained permission to attend his brother's funeral and used the occasion to run from the police. He was only twenty, but as he wandered through the backstreets of Buenos Aires, he lost his will to live. That's when he met a Christian boy who began telling him about the power of following Christ. When Adrián turned from his sins to receive Christ as Savior, something happened within him. He became a man on fire for the Lord. He enrolled at the Word of Life Bible Institute in San Miguel del Monte, and he developed a faith as precious as Peter's. He felt the currents of God's divine power and began learning about His precious promises. As he studied God's Word, he began building the eight essential characteristics necessary for a life of confidence—the very qualities we've been studying.

Today Adrián, along with his wife and daughter, have a ministry for people battling AIDS and self-destructive behaviors in Latin America. He speaks in high schools and assemblies throughout Argentina and in thirty-five other countries around the world. "I tell young people everywhere to bypass the path of drugs, so they don't suffer the torment I endured. And I tell them about the gospel of Christ, the only thing with the power to transform a life."[2]

Believe me, the Lord can transform your life too. Today Jesus is saying to you, "Follow Me."

I implore you to place your faith in Him and let Him give you a faith as precious as Peter's. Make that decision right now and pray something like this:

Dear Lord, I confess my faults and failures—my sins—and repent of them. Here and now, I ask Jesus Christ to come into my life. I want to follow Him. Give me a faith as precious as Peter's, and help me build a life of spiritual strength by adding to my faith the Christlike qualities You desire in me. And may I keep growing in the grace and knowledge of the Lord Jesus Christ until that day when I receive a rich welcome into the eternal kingdom of God. I pray this in Jesus' name. Amen!

May God bless you as you follow Him! And never forget: He's already given you *everything you need!*

Salvation is found in no one else, for there is no other name under heaven given to mankind by which we must be saved (Acts 4:12 NIV).
—SIMON PETER

ACKNOWLEDGMENTS

Every day of my life I have the privilege of devoting my time and energy to the only two things in the whole world that are eternal: the Word of God and people. I am so blessed to be surrounded by a team that is deeply committed to these two priorities.

At the center of that team is my wife Donna, whose office is right next to mine and whose heart has been next to mine for fifty-six years. Together we have dreamed and planned and worked toward the goal of influencing our world for Christ. More than ever before we have been seeing our dreams come true.

My oldest son, David Michael is our managing partner at Turning Point Ministries. His role continues to expand each year, and it is because he has taken so much off of my administrative plate that I am able to produce books like the one you have just read. There are no words to describe the joy that is mine as I have the privilege to work with my son every day. At first, I was teaching him but now, it seems to me, I am learning from him . . . especially about his generation, which is so different from mine.

Diane Sutherland is my administrative assistant at our international headquarters, and she coordinates my schedule, my travel, my partnerships . . . basically my life! Diane is much loved and respected by all of us at Turning Point and by people all over the world who interact with her on our behalf. To so many people, Diane is Turning Point.

Beau Sager is the coordinator of research and editing. He provides considerable research himself and also works with our team to assure that our information is timely and accurate. Beau is a stickler for details and one of the most godly, diligent, hardworking, servant-hearted men I have ever known.

At the beginning stages of the project, Tom Williams helped us get momentum. Thank you, Tom, for your willingness to lend your creative hand to this book.

Rob Morgan has worked with me at Turning Point for many years, and I am constantly amazed at his ability to get inside my head and my heart so that whatever he brings to our projects is exactly what we need. If this book arrives at the goal we set for it, Rob Morgan will be one of the main reasons.

Jennifer Hansen is the newest member of our publication team. She has a long and distinguished background as a writer and editor and her contributions to the final draft of this manuscript made this book so much better. Thank you, Jennifer, for making time to help us.

The people I have just mentioned were totally involved in the publication of *Everything You Need*, but there is so much more to a book than its mere release. The promotion, marketing, and circulation efforts of both the author and his team, and the publisher's team, determines the fate of the book.

Our creative department led by Paul Joiner is second to none in the development and deployment of the finest and most up-to-date marketing and promotional strategies being utilized today. Everyone who has seen Paul's work agrees with my assessment. Paul Joiner is one of God's best gifts to Turning Point.

ACKNOWLEDGMENTS

And this year we have once again had the privilege of teaming up with Mark Schoenwald, Daisy Hutton, Sam O'Neal, and the W Publishing team. More and more, with each book, we are finding creative ways to work together so that our message can reach as many readers as possible.

As with all my other writing projects, I am represented by Sealy Yates of Yates and Yates. We consider Sealy, his whole family, and his business associates members of our Turning Point team. We have watched as God has honored this relationship now for over twenty-five years.

None of us deserves to have our names on the same page with the name of our Lord and Savior, Jesus Christ. This is really all about Him! This is His message! We are His messengers! Whatever glory comes from this endeavor belongs to Him and Him alone. He alone is worthy!

David Jeremiah
San Diego, California—July 2019

NOTES

PROLOGUE

1. Douglas Main, "How the World's Deepest Fish Survives Bone-Crushing Pressure," *National Geographic*, April 15, 2019, https://www.nationalgeographic.com/animals/2019/04/how-deep-sea-snailfish-survive-mariana-trench/.

CHAPTER 1: THE PROMISE

1. Agueda Pacheco-Flores, "German Hitchhiker, Stuck on the Pacific Crest Trail, Saved by a Stranger," *The Seattle Times,* October 31, 2018, https://www.seattletimes.com/seattle-news/german-hiker-stuck-on-the-pacific-crest-trail-saved-by-a-stranger/.
2. "How Much Energy Does the Sun Produce?" *Boston Globe*, September 5, 2005, https://archive.boston.com/news/science/articles/2005/09/05/how_much_energy_does_the_sun_produce/.
3. "Knowledge Is Power," *Project Gutenberg*, accessed May 15, 2019, https://www.gutenberg.us/articles/knowledge_is_power.
4. "The 13-Year-Old Boy Who Stole a Bus to Help His Family," *BBC News*, November 10, 2017, https://www.bbc.com/news/stories-41764829.
5. Everek R. Storms, "Standing on the Promises," *Contact Magazine*, March, 1978, 13–14.
6. Adapted and used with permission from Robert J. Morgan, *All to Jesus: A Year of Devotions* (Nashville, TN: B&H Publishing Group, 2012), Day 168.

7. Matt Saintsing, "A Search, a Book, and a Promise Kept 50 Years Later," *Radio.com*, April 2, 2019, https://connectingvets.radio.com/articles /thomas-bragg-keeps-promise-he-made-eddie-lama-vietnam-50-years-ago.

8. Jeff Clark, "Why Is Gold Valuable? The 5 Reasons Most Investors Overlook," *Hard Assets Alliance*, October 7, 2015, https://www .hardassetsalliance.com/blog/why-is-gold-valuable-the-5-reasons -most-investors-overlook#.

9. Adapted from Tony Evans, *Tony Evans' Book of Illustrations* (Chicago, IL: Moody Publishers, 2009), 24–25.

10. Amber Angelle, "Why Do Couples Start to Look Like Each Other," *Live Science*, June 20, 2010, https://www.livescience.com/8384-couples-start. html and Jamie Ducharme, "Why Do So Many Couples Look Alike," *Time*, April 4, 2019, https://time.com/5553817/couples-who-look-alike/.

11. See Hebrews 12:1 (KJV), *BibleGateway*, accessed July 9, 2019, https://www. biblegateway.com/passage/?search=Hebrews+12%3A1&version=KJV.

12. Zoe Szathmary, "Georgia Teacher Donates Kidney to 12-Year-Old Student," *Fox News*, August 14, 2018, https://www.foxnews.com/ health/georgia-teacher-donates-kidney-to-12-year-old-student and Helena Oliviero, "Updated: Local Teacher Donates Kidney to Teacher," *Atlanta Journal-Constitution*, August 14, 2018, https://www.ajc.com/ lifestyles/local-teacher-donates-kidney-student/18FwjPfsGJeZsP6rCc 7BdL/. See also "Kaden's Kidney Search," https://www.facebook.com/ kadenskidneysearch/.

CHAPTER 2: MUSCULAR FAITH

1. "Read: George W. Bush's Eulogy at His Father's Funeral," *CNN*, December 5, 2018, https://www.cnn.com/2018/12/05/politics/george-w -bush-eulogy-hw-bush-funeral/index.html.

2. Eric W. Hayden, "Did You Know?" *The Spurgeon Archive*, accessed April 29, 2019, https://archive.spurgeon.org/spurgn2.php.

3. Charles Haddon Spurgeon, *Spurgeon's Sermons Volume 8: 1863* (Ontario, Canada: Devoted Publishing, 2017), 179.

4. Charles Spurgeon, *Metropolitan Tabernacle Pulpit*, "The Great Sin of Doing Nothing," accessed April 4, 2019, https://www.spurgeongems.org /vols31–33/chs1916.pdf.

5. See Douglas J. Moo, *The NIV Application Commentary: 2 Peter, Jude* (Grand Rapids, MI: Zondervan, 1996), 44.

6. "Diligence," *Merriam-Webster*, accessed May 7, 2019, https://www.merriam-webster.com/dictionary/diligence.

7. "Diligence," *Webster's Dictionary 1828—Online Edition*, accessed April 4, 2019, https://webstersdictionary1828.com/Dictionary/diligent.

8. Andreas J. Köstenberger, *Excellence: The Character of God and the Pursuit of Scholarly Virtue* (Wheaton, IL: Crossway, 2011), 88.

9. J. Allen Blair, *A Devotional Study of the Second Epistle of Peter* (New York, NY: Loizeaux Brothers, 1961), 30.

10. Darrah Brustein, "Ventriloquist Terry Fator on Why 'Overnight Success' Is a Myth," *Forbes*, April 21, 2019, https://www.forbes.com/sites/darrahbrustein/2019/04/21/ventriloquist-terry-fator-on-why-overnight-success-is-a-myth/#1550b18b218a.

11. Dr. Sydney Ceruto, "The Neuroscience of Motivation: How Our Brains Drive Hard Work and Achievement," *Forbes*, March 26, 2019, https://www.forbes.com/sites/forbescoachescouncil/2019/03/26/the-neuroscience-of-motivation-how-our-brains-drive-hard-work-and-achievement/#aafd10d5fcba.

12. Noah Trister, "Power, Penske Collect Indy 500 Trophies," *StarTribune*, January 17, 2019, https://www.startribune.com/power-penske-collect-indy-500-trophies/504461922/.

13. William Barclay, *The Letters of James and Peter*, rev. ed. (Philadelphia, PA: Westminster, 1976), 298–99.

14. Clayborne Carson, ed., *The Papers of Martin Luther King Jr.: Volume IV: The Symbol of Movement January 1957-December 1958* (Berkeley, CA: University of California Press, 2000), 79.

15. Angela Duckworth, *Grit: The Power of Passion and Perseverance* (New York, NY: Scribner, 2016), 8.

16. Ibid., 132.

17. Marshall Shelley, "To Illustrate," *Christianity Today*, accessed June 4, 2019, https://www.christianitytoday.com/pastors/1984/fall/84l4046.html.

18. Marsha DuCille, "God Will See," *Called Magazine*, accessed July 9, 2019, https://www.calledmagazine.com/devotionals/item/184-god-will-see.

19. Johanna Li and Leigh Scheps, "Former Member of Elvis Presley's Inner Circle Faces Foreclosure Due to Mounting Medical Bills," *Inside Edition*, December 2, 2016, https://www.insideedition.com/headlines/20228-former-member-of-elvis-presleys-inner-circle-faces-foreclosure-due-to-mounting-medical-bills.

20. Charles Spurgeon, "For the Sick and Afflicted," *The Spurgeon Archive*, accessed May 13, 2019, https://archive.spurgeon.org/sermons/1274.php.

CHAPTER 3: MORAL EXCELLENCE

1. Nathan Resnick, "Interview with Tim Nybo: The Story of Vincero Watches," *Sourcify*, June 12, 2018, https://www.sourcify.com/tim-nybo -vincero-watches-multimillion-dollar-brand/. See also Tim Nybo, Aaron Hallerman, and Sean Agatep, "The Vincero Origin Story," *Vincero*, accessed May 31, 2019, https://vincerowatches.com/pages/the-vincero -story.

2. Tim Nybo, "Chinese Manufacturing: A Crash Course in Quality Control," *Forbes*, February 21, 2019, https://www.forbes.com/sites /theyec/2019/02/21/chinese-manufacturing-a-crash-course-in-qualit y-control/#79ec600975ae.

3. Abbas Hameed, "How God Sent His Word to an Iraqi Interpreter," *Christianity Today*, June 21, 2017, https://www.christianitytoday.com /ct/2017/july-august/how-god-sent-his-word-to-iraqi-interpreter.html.

4. Elizabeth Hoagland, *Let's Be Friends* (Bloomington, IN: WestBow Press, 2018), 143–44.

5. Pat Williams and Jim Denney, *How to Be Like Walt: Capturing the Disney Magic Every Day in Your Life* (Deerfield Beach, FL: Health Communication, Inc., 2004), 92.

6. Wess Stafford, *Just a Minute* (Chicago, IL: Moody Press, 2012), 37.

7. "What Tiger Said in His Masters Winner's Press Conference," *Golf Channel Digital*, April 14, 2019, https://www.golfchannel.com/news /what-tiger-woods-said-his-2019-masters-winners-press-conference.

8. Kevin DeYoung, "Yes, You Can Please Your Heavenly Father," *The Gospel Coalition*, March 9, 2017, https://www.thegospelcoalition.org/blogs/kevin -deyoung/yes-you-can-please-your-father/.

9. Randy Alcorn, *The Purity Principle* (Colorado Springs, CO: Multnomah Books, 2003), 9–10.

10. "Accountability Partner," *Wikipedia*, accessed June 1, 2019, https://en .wikipedia.org/wiki/Accountability_partner.

11. Johnny Hunt, *The Gift of Jesus* (Nashville, TN: Thomas Nelson, 2015), 48.

12. Megan Mertz, "Spring 'Engage': Brought Together in Christ," *Reporter*, April 15, 2019, https://blogs.lcms.org/2019/spring-engage-brought -together-in-christ/.

13. *The Bible Knowledge Commentary: New Testament* (Colorado Springs, CO: Victor, 2000), 703.

14. Good News Network, "When Driver Sees Cash Flying Through Air on the Highway, She Turns it All in to Grateful Widow," *Good News Network*, February 8, 2019, https://www.goodnewsnetwork.org/when-driver-sees -cash-flying-through-the-air-on-the-highway-she-turns-it-all-in-to -grateful-widow/.

15. Louis Albert Banks, *The Religious Life of Famous Americans* (New York, NY: American Tract Society, 1904), 69.

CHAPTER 4: MENTAL FOCUS

1. Katherine Rosenberg-Douglas, "Great-grandfather, 90, Set to Become Northeastern Illinois University's Oldest Confirmed Graduate," *Chicago Tribune*, April 29, 2019, https://www.chicagotribune.com/news/ct-me t-great-grandfather-oldest-northeastern-illinois-graduate-20190426 -story.html.

2. Attributed to Benjamin Franklin.

3. NPR Staff, "Meet William James Sidis: The Smartest Guy Ever?," *NPR*, January 23, 2011, https://www.npr.org/2011/01/23/132737060/meet -william-james-sidis-the-smartest-guy-ever. See also "William James Sidis," *Wikipedia*, accessed May 31, 2019, https://en.wikipedia.org/wiki /William_James_Sidis.

4. Rosalind Picard, "An MIT Professor Meets the Author of All Knowledge," *Christianity Today*, March 15, 2019, https://www.christianitytoday.com /ct/2019/april/rosalind-picard-mit-professor-meets-author-knowledge .html.

5. Ruth Bell Graham, *It's My Turn* (Old Tappan, NJ: Fleming H. Revell Company, 1982), 170.

6. Sarah Eekhoff Zylstra, "What the Latest Bible Research Reveals about Millennials," *Christianity Today*, May 16, 2016, https://www .christianitytoday.com/news/2016/may/what-latest-bible-research -reveals-about-millennials.html.

7. Kate Lamb, "Indonesian Teenager's Ocean Ordeal," *The Guardian*, September 28, 2018, https://www.theguardian.com/world/2018/sep /28/indonesian-teenagers-ocean-ordeal-after-a-week-i-started-to -get-scared.

8. Skip Hollandsworth, "Faith, Friendship, and Tragedy at Santa Fe High,"

Texas Monthly, May 2019, https://www.texasmonthly.com/articles
/remembering-sabika-sheikh-pakistani-student-killed-santa-fe-school
-shooting/.

9. Charles Chandler, "The Bible's Immeasurable Impact," *Billy Graham
Evangelistic Association*, September 14, 2017, https://billygraham.org
/decision-magazine/september-2017/the-bibles-immeasurable-impact/.

10. Betty Lee Skinner, *Daws: A Man Who Trusted God* (Grand Rapid, MI:
Zondervan, 1974), 26–31.

11. Karen Drew, "Michigan Man Learns Meteorite He's Been Using as a
Doorstop Is Worth $100,000," *Click on Detroit*, October 5, 2018, https://
www.clickondetroit.com/news/michigan-man-learns-meteorite-hes-been
-using-as-doorstop-is-worth-100000.

CHAPTER 5: PERSONAL DISCIPLINE

1. Ann Killion, "Give Draymond Green Jr. an Assist for His Dad's Improved
Behavior," *San Francisco Chronicle*, May 19, 2019, https://www.sfchronicle.
com/sports/annkillion/article/Give-Draymond-Jr-an-assist-for-Dad-s
-improved-13857775.php.

2. Heloise, "Hints from Heloise: No Discipline?," *The Washington Post*,
May 13, 2019, . https://www.washingtonpost.com/lifestyle/style/hints
-from-heloise-no-discipline/2019/05/09/a5f1e2bc-6b68–11e9–8f44
-e8d8bb1df986_story.html?utm_term=.1a3442bef1bc.

3. Randy Frazee, *Think, Act, Be Like Jesus* (Grand Rapids, MI: Zondervan,
2014), 184.

4. Tom Porter, "Profile of a Busy Senior," *Bowdoin*, May 6, 2019, https://
www.bowdoin.edu/news/2019/05/profile-of-a-busy-senior-amir-parker
-19-juggles-army-track-math-and-philosophy.html.

5. Barbara Hughes, *Disciplines of a Godly Woman* (Wheaton, IL: Crossway
Books, 2001), 11–12.

6. Randy Frazee, 184–85.

7. C. S. Lewis, *God in the Dock* (Grand Rapids, MI: Eerdmans: 1970), 216.

8. Adapted from Maria Konnikova, "The Struggles of a Psychologist
Studying Self-Control," *The New Yorker*, October 9, 2014, https://www
.newyorker.com/science/maria-konnikova/struggles-psychologist-
studying-self-control.

9. Natasha Frost, "The Founder of the Famous Marshmallow Test Had Some
Great Advice About Self-Control," *Quartz*, September 14, 2018, https://qz

.com/1390515/walter-mischel-the-marshmallow-test-founder-had-great
-tips-on-self-control/.

10. Neil Petch, "What Real Discipline Looks Like," *Entrepreneur*, August 28, 2016, https://www.entrepreneur.com/article/281542. See also Lucas Reilly, "How Stephen King's Wife Saved Carrie and Launched His Career," *Mental Floss*, January 11, 2017, https://mentalfloss.com/article/53235 /how-stephen-kings-wife-saved-carrie-and-launched-his-career.

11. "Life Lessons and War Stories from Admiral William H. McRaven," *CBS News*, May 12, 2019, https://www.cbsnews.com/news/life-lessons-and-war -stories-from-admiral-william-h-mcraven/.

12. Shana Lebowitz, "The Most 'Disciplined' People Don't Have More Self-Control Than You—They Just Make a Different Daily Choice," *Business Insider*, November 11, 2018, https://www.businessinsider.com/discipline -avoiding-temptation-science-2018–11.

13. Lindsay Abrams, "Study: People with a Lot of Self-Control Are Happier," *The Atlantic*, July 1, 2013, https://www.theatlantic.com/health/archive /2013/07/study-people-with-a-lot-of-self-control-are-happier/277349/.

14. Mark Twain, *The Writings of Mark Twain* (United States of America, 1899), 158.

15. Quin Sherrer and Ruthanne Garlock, *You Can Break That Habit and Be Free* (Ada, MI: Baker Publishing Group, 2012), 15–17.

16. Joe Middleton, "Boris Becker's Treasured Tennis Trophies and Memorabilia Will Be Sold," *Daily Mail*, May 21, 2019, https://www .dailymail.co.uk/news/article-7054741/Boris-Beckers-treasured -tennis-trophies-memorabilia-sold-1m-June-auction.html. See also Ruth Brown, "How playboy tennis legend Boris Becker lost it all," *New York Post,* June 21, 2017, https://nypost.com/2017/06/21 /how-playboy-tennis-legend-boris-becker-lost-it-all/.

17. Story adapted from a personal interview.

CHAPTER 6: RELENTLESS DETERMINATION

1. Adapted from David L. Allen, "My All-Time Favorite Sports Sermon Illustration!," March 13, 2019, https://drdavidlallen.com/sermons/my-all -time-favorite-sports-sermon-illustration/. See also Julietta Jameson, *Cliffy: The Cliff Young Story* (Melbourne, Australia: Text Publishing, 2013).

2. See Douglas J. Moo, *The NIV Application Commentary: 2 Peter, Jude* (Grand Rapids, MI: Zondervan Publishing House, 1996), 46.

3. Eugene Peterson, *A Long Obedience in the Same Direction* (Downers Grove, IL: InterVarsity Press, 2000), 131–32.

4. Adapted from "Byron Janis (Piano)," accessed March 27, 2019, https://www.bach-cantatas.com/Bio/Janis-Byron.htm.

5. Ibid.

6. Dena Yohe, *You Are Not Alone* (New York, NY: WaterBrook, 2016), 12, 121.

7. Chris Tiegreen, *The One Year Walk with God Devotional* (Wheaton, IL: Tyndale House Publishers, Inc., 2004), March 6.

8. Adapted from Omee Thao, "Difficult Journey Leads to Blessed Life," *Alliance*, accessed March 30, 2019, https://www.cmalliance.org/news/2015/04/09/difficult-journey-leads-to-blessed-life/.

9. Joni Eareckson Tada, *Heaven: Your Real Home* (Grand Rapids, MI: Zondervan, 2018), 171.

10. Gerri Willis, "Breast Cancer Taught Me to Live Day by Day, Hour by Hour," *Good Housekeeping*, October 27, 2017, https://www.goodhousekeeping.com/health/a46636/gerri-willis-breast-cancer/.

11. Peter Rosenberger, *Hope for the Caregiver* (Nashville, TN: Worthy Publishing Group, 2014), 99–100.

12. Adapted from Eun Kyung Kim, "Inspiring 3-Year-Old Twins with Down Syndrome Have Become Social Media Stars," *Today*, March 27, 2019, https://www.today.com/parents/inspiring-3-year-old-twins-down-syndrome-have-become-social-t151064?cid=public-rss_20190328.

13. Erin Clements, "Every Single Thing I Know, as of Today': Author Anne Lamott Shares Life Wisdom in Viral Facebook Post," *Today*, April 9, 2015, https://www.today.com/popculture/author-anne-lamott-shares-life-wisdom-viral-facebook-post-t13881.

14. Zoë Read, "Daughter of Fallen Wilmington Firefighter Receives National Scholarship," *Why*, February 5, 2019, https://whyy.org/articles/daughter-of-fallen-wilmington-firefighter-receives-national-scholarship/.

15. Helen Wilbers, "Record-Setting Hiker Shares Lesson," *News Tribune*, May 27, 2018, https://www.newstribune.com/news/local/story/2018/may/27/learning-on-her-feet/728085/.

16. Stephanie Gallman, "Elite Runner Crawls Across the Finish Line at Austin Marathon," *CNN*, February 17, 2015, https://www.cnn.com/2015/02/16/us/austin-marathon-finish-line-crawl/index.html.

17. "Runners Inspired by Crawl to Finish Line," *CBS Austin*, February 16,

2015, https://cbsaustin.com/sports/content/runners-inspired-by-crawl
-to-finish-line.

CHAPTER 7: CHRISTLIKE CHARACTER

1. Eric Todsico, "Perpetrator Breaks into Massachusetts Home—And Cleans It Thoroughly," *People*, May 24, 2019, https://people.com/human-interes t/house-broken-into-cleaned/.

2. Craig Groeschel, *Soul Detox: Clean Living in a Contaminated World* (Grand Rapids, MI: Zondervan, 2012), 14, 18.

3. Milledge L. Bonham Jr., "James Butler Bonham: A Consistent Rebel," *Southwestern Historical Quarterly*, vol. 35, 136.

4. Tim Stebbins, "LeBron James Says Meeting Michael Joran for the First Time Was 'Godly,'" *NBC Sports*, December 15, 2018, https://www .nbcsports.com/chicago/bulls/lebron-james-says-meeting-michael-jordan -first-time-was-godly.

5. Janet Holm McHenry, "I Never Felt Special," *Looking Up*, February 25, 2019, https://janetmchenry.com/lookingup/2019/02/25/i-never-felt -special/.

6. Donald Whitney, "10 Questions to Ask to Make Sure You're Still Growing," *C. S. Lewis Institute*, December 15, 2013, https://www .cslewisinstitute.org/10_Questions_To_Ask_To_Make_Sure_Youre _Still_Growing_page4.

7. Eric Metaxas, "Christ in the Nuba Mountains," *Breakpoint*, July 23, 2015, https://www.breakpoint.org/2015/07/christ-nuba-mountains/. See also Nicholas Kristof, "He's Jesus Christ," *New York Times,* June 27, 2015, https://www.nytimes.com/2015/06/28/opinion/sunday/nicholas-kristof -hes-jesus-christ.html.

8. Kristin Crawford, "Hometown Hero: Daniel Blevins Takes Hurricane Relief Efforts into His Own Hands," *WECT News*, November 30, 2018, https://www.wect.com/2018/11/30/hometown-hero-daniel-blevins-takes -hurricane-relief-efforts-into-his-own-hands/.

9. Caleb Parke, "Coffee with a Cause," *Fox News*, May 21, 2019, https://www .foxnews.com/faith-values/coffee-video-christian-company-single -mom-car.

10. Brian S. Rosner, *Known by God: A Biblical Theology of Personal Identity* (Grand Rapids, MI: Zondervan, 2017), 22–23.

11. Ed Stetzer, "One-on-One with Brian Rosner on Known by God: A Biblical

Theology of Personal Identity," *Christianity Today*, March 22, 2018, https://www.christianitytoday.com/edstetzer/2018/march/one-on-one -with-brian-rosner-on-known-by-god-biblical-theol.html.

12. Julie Beck, "'For-Now Parents' and 'Big Feelings': How Sesame Street Talks Trauma," *Atlantic*, May 20, 2019, https://www.theatlantic.com/family /archive/2019/05/sesame-street-created-foster-care-muppet/589756/.

13. Original source uncertain.

14. John Jessup, "'I Wanna See Jesus, but Not Right Now': Boy's Face Impaled by 17-inch Skewer, How He Miraculously Survived," *CBN News*, September 28, 2018, https://www1.cbn.com/cbnnews/us/2018/september /i-wanna-see-jesus-but-not-right-now-boys-face-impaled-by-17-inch -skewer-how-he-miraculously-survived.

15. Angela Andaloro, "First look at Renée Zellweger as Judy Garland for Upcoming Film About the Troubled Actress' Life," *Little Things*, accessed May 16, 2019, https://www.littlethings.com/renee-zellweger -judy-garland-biopic-first-look.

16. Charlene Aaron, "'I Just Felt the Holy Spirit Speak to Me': Man Stops Dramatic Suicide in Progress, Leads Jumper to Christ," *CBN News*, May 17, 2019, https://www1.cbn.com/cbnnews/us/2019/may/i-just -felt-the-holy-spirit-speak-to-me-man-stops-dramatic-suicide-in -progress-leads-jumper-to-christ.

CHAPTER 8: RADICAL KINDNESS

1. Otillia Steadman, "A Beloved Mail Carrier Retired and the Whole Neighborhood Turned Out to Say Goodbye," *Buzzfeed News*, May 24, 2019, https://www.buzzfeednews.com/article/otilliasteadman /georgia-mailman-retires-floyd-martin. See also Caitlin O'Kane, "Entire Community Honors Beloved Mailman on His Last Day of Work," *CBS News*, May 28, 2019, https://www.cbsnews.com/news /marietta-georgia-community-honors-beloved-mailman-floyd -martin-on-his-last-day-of-work-2019–05–28/. See also McKinley Corbley, "After Mailman Puts Off Retirement Out of Love for Neighbors, Hundreds of People Send Him on Dream Vacation," *Good News Network*, May 30, 2019, https://www.goodnewsnetwork .org/people-send-beloved-atlanta-mailman-to-hawaii/.

2. Tyler Huckabee, "'Won't You Be My Neighbor' Explores the Radical Kindness of 'Mister Rogers' Neighborhood,'" *Relevant*, June 11, 2018,

https://relevantmagazine.com/culture/film/wont-you-be-my-neighbor
-explores-the-radical-kindness-of-mister-rogers-neighborhood/.

3. Jessica Napoli, "Joanna Gaines Celebrates 16th Anniversary to Chip
with Sweet Post," *Fox News*, June 2, 2019, https://www.foxnews.com
/entertainment/joanna-chip-gaines-celebrate-16th-wedding-anniversary.

4. Stormie Omartian, *The Power of a Praying Wife* (Eugene, OR: Harvest
House Publishers, 1997), 34.

5. "Hero Biker Helps Father Get Unconscious Daughter to the Hospital
Through Heavy Traffic," *Sunny Skyz*, May 31, 2019, https://www
.sunnyskyz.com/good-news/3338/Hero-Biker-Helps-Father-Get
-Unconscious-Daughter-To-The-Hospital-Through-Heavy-Traffic.

6. Frederick Buechner, *Wishful Thinking: A Theological ABC* (New York,
NY: Harper & Row, 1973), 2.

7. Annie Chapman, *Letting Go of Anger* (Eugene, OR: Harvest House, 2000),
7–10.

8. McKinley Corbley, "After Policeman Gives Wandering Child Ride Home,
He Returns with Groceries and Treats for the Family," *Good News
Network*, June 12, 2019, https://www.goodnewsnetwork.org/after
-policeman-gives-child-ride-home-he-returns-with-groceries/.

9. Alexandria Hein, "Nurse Adopts Girl Who Had No Visitors During
Hospital Stay," *Fox News*, April 5, 2019, https://www.foxnews.com/health
/nurse-adopts-infant-who-had-no-visitors-during-hospital-stay. See
also "Liz & Gisele's Story," *Franciscan Children's*, accessed June 19, 2019,
https://franciscanchildrens.org/our-stories/liz-giseles-story/.

10. John Galt, *The Life and Studies of Benjamin West* (London, England: T.
Candell and W. Davies, 1817), 9–11.

11. Barbara Maranzani, "What Abraham Lincoln Was Carrying in His
Pockets the Night He Was Killed," *Biography*, June 10, 2019, https://www
.biography.com/news/abraham-lincoln-pockets-assassination. See also
Greg Asimakoupoulos, "Icons Every Pastor Needs," *Christianity Today*,
accessed June 19, 2019, https://www.christianitytoday.com/pastors/1993
/winter/93l4108.html.

12. "An Entire School Learned Sign Language to Welcome a Deaf
Kindergartener," *Sunny Skyz*, June 2, 2019, https://www.sunnyskyz.com
/good-news/3340/An-Entire-School-Learned-Sign-Language-To
-Welcome-A-Deaf-Kindergartener.

13. Caitlin O'Kane, "63 Years After Being Expelled: First Black University

of Alabama Student Gets Honorary Degree," *WFMY News*, May 7, 2019, https://www.wfmynews2.com/article/news/nation-world/63-years-after -being-expelled-first-black-university-of-alabama-student-gets-honorary -degree/83–66b9890e-6e8d-469a-ae75-b19b920e9e92.

14. McKinley Corbley, "When Woman Shares Photo of Anonymous Gift Found in a Book, It Sparks Chain of Good Deeds," *Good News Network*, May 7, 2019, https://www.goodnewsnetwork.org/anonymous-gift-found -in-book-sparks-chain-of-good-deeds/.

15. Ben Hooper, "Irish Students Break Back-Patting World Record," *UPI*, May 31, 2019, https://www.upi.com/Odd_News/2019/05/31/Irish -students-break-back-patting-world-record/5201559315580/.

16. Caitlin Keating, "Florida Mailman, 60, Spends His Days Off Cleaning Veterans' Headstones at Rundown Cemeteries," *People*, May 30, 2019, https://people.com/human-interest/florida-mailman-cleans-veterans -headstones/.

17. Quoted by Annie Chapman, *Letting Go of Anger* (Eugene, OR: Harvest House, 2000), 45.

18. Chris Brauns, *Unpacking Forgiveness* (Wheaton, IL: Crossway Books, 2008), 25–29.

19. Capi Lynn, "Inmates Repay Prison Officer Randy Geer's Compassion in His Hour of Need," *Statesman Journal*, June 19, 2019, https://www .statesmanjournal.com/story/news/2019/06/19/penitentiary-inmates -repay-kindness-department-of-corrections-officer/1426450001/.

CHAPTER 9: SELFLESS LOVE

1. The wording of these plaques has been slightly edited for readability.

2. Mike Dash, "On Heroic Self-Sacrifice: A London Park Devoted to Those Most Worth Remembering," *Smithsonian*, March 19, 2012, https://www .smithsonianmag.com/history/on-heroic-self-sacrifice-a-london-park -devoted-to-those-most-worth-remembering-129818509/. See also *London Remembers*, accessed June 25, 2019, https://www.londonremembers.com /memorials/pp-3w-bristow.

3. Mike Yaconelli, "The Author of Messy Spirituality Discusses God's Annoying Love," *Christianity Today*, August 1, 2002, https://www .christianitytoday.com/ct/2002/augustweb-only/8–5–21.0.html.

4. "Like Angels Sent By God," *Samaritan's Purse*, May 30, 2019, https://www .samaritanspurse.org/article/like-angels-sent-by-god/.

5. Barbara Diamond, "Sad Homeless Man Sits On Same Corner for 3 Years, Until Curious Mom Pulls Up to Ask Him Why," *Little Things*, accessed June 25, 2019, https://www.littlethings.com/homeless-man-victor/4. See also Story Team, "This is Ginger," *Clear Creek Community Church*, accessed July 10, 2019, https://www.clearcreekstories.org/this-is-ginger/. See also Billy Hallowell, "'She Kind of Saved Me': Homeless Man's Life Is Totally Transformed After Woman's Simple Act of Goodness," *Faithwire*, March 16, 2017, https://www.faithwire.com/2017/03/16/she-kind-of-saved -me-homeless-mans-life-is-totally-transformed-after-womans-simple-act -of-goodness/.

6. "A Chef Has Been Delivering Free Soup to a Stranger for Over a Year," *Sunny Skyz*, May 13, 2019, https://www.sunnyskyz.com/good-news /3314/A-Chef-Has-Been-Delivering-Free-Soup-To-A-Stranger-With-MS -For-Over-A-Year.

7. Jon Bloom, "If We Love God Most, We Will Love Others Best," *Desiring God*, June 24, 2016, https://www.desiringgod.org/articles/if-we-love-god -most-we-will-love-others-best.

8. Quoted in Philip Carlson, *You Were Made for Love* (Colorado Springs, CO: Life Journey, 2006), 175–176.

9. Paco Amador, "Weeping with Gang Members," *Christianity Today*, accessed June 25, 2019, https://www.christianitytoday.com/pastors/2014 /winter/weeping-on-heavens-behalf.html.

10. Becky Kopitzke, *Generous Love: Discover the Joy of Living "Others First"* (Bloomington, MN: Bethany House Publishers, 2018), 181–82.

11. Judy Douglass, "The Lived-Out Gospel," *Family Life*, accessed June 25, 2019, https://www.familylife.com/articles/topics/faith/essentials-faith /reaching-out/the-lived-out-gospel/.

12. John Piper, "The Greatest of These Is Love: An Introduction to the Series," *Desiring God*, March 12, 1995, https://www.desiringgod.org/messages /the-greatest-of-these-is-love-an-introduction-to-the-series.

13. Henry Drummond, *The Greatest Thing in the World* (Kila, MT: Kessinger Publishing, 1998), 27.

14. Adapted from Greg Asimakoupoulos, "Hearing God's Word of Love," *Preaching Today*, accessed June 25, 2019, https://www.preachingtoday.com /illustrations/2002/january/13448.html.

15. Caitlin Keating, "Ohio Officer Saves Six Lives Within Two Hours: 'You Never Know What's in Store for You,'" *People*, June 13, 2019, https://

people.com/human-interest/ohio-officer-saves-six-lives-within-two
-hours/.

CHAPTER 10: THE BLESSING

1. Gale Rosenblum, "Retired St. Paul Cop Melvin Carter Jr. Helps Young Black Men Rewrite Their Script," *StarTribune*, June 10,2019, https://www .startribune.com/former-st-paul-cop-and-mentor-melvin-carter-jr-helps -young-black-men-rewrite-their-script/510974632/.

2. "Decorations for His Glory," *The Christian Heart*, June 24, 2019, https:// www.thechristianheart.com/decorations-for-his-glory/.

3. "Raising Men Lawn Care Service," *The Christian Heart*, August 22, 2018, https://www.thechristianheart.com/raising-men-lawn-care-service/.

4. Zane Hodges, "Making Your Calling and Election Sure: An Exposition of 2 Peter 1:5–11," *Journal of the Grace Evangelical Society*, Vol. 11.1, 1998, np.

5. Ibid.

6. Jonathan Aitken, *John Newton* (Wheaton, IL: Crossway Books, 2007), 347.

7. John MacArthur, "The Key to Spiritual Stability in the Christian Life," *Crossway*, February 26, 2015, https://www.crossway.org/articles/the-key -to-spiritual-stability-in-the-christian-life/.

8. Gretchen Saffles, "Finding Stability in Transition," *Well-Watered Women Co.*, November 14, 2017, https://wellwateredwomen.com/staying-stable -in-transition/.

9. J. D. Greear, *Stop Asking Jesus Into Your Heart: How to Know for Sure You Are Saved* (Nashville, TN: B&H Publishing, 2013), 2–3.

10. Ronald Reagan, *An American Life* (New York, NY: Simon &Schuster, 1990), chapter 3.

11. David Jeremiah, *Living with Confidence in a Chaotic World* (Nashville, TN: Thomas Nelson, 2009), 87.

EPILOGUE

1. Gyles Brandreth, *The Joy of Lex: How to Have Fun with 860,341,500 Words* (New York, NY: William Morrow & Co., 1983).

2. Based on personal correspondence with Word of Life International. Used with permission.

ABOUT THE AUTHOR

David Jeremiah is the founder of Turning Point, an international ministry committed to providing Christians with sound Bible teaching through radio and television, the Internet, live events, and resource materials and books. He is the author of more than fifty books, including *Overcomer, Is This the End?, The Spiritual Warfare Answer Book, David Jeremiah Morning and Evening Devotions, Airship Genesis Kids Study Bible,* and *The Jeremiah Study Bible.*

Dr. Jeremiah serves as the senior pastor of Shadow Mountain Community Church in San Diego, California, where he resides with his wife, Donna. They have four grown children and twelve grandchildren. Learn more at DavidJeremiah.org.

FURTHER YOUR STUDY OF THIS BOOK

• • • • • • • •

Everything You Need Resource Materials

To enhance your study on this important topic, we recommend the correlating audio message album, study guide, and DVD messages from the *Everything You Need* series.

Audio Message Album

The material found in this book originated from messages presented by Dr. Jeremiah at Shadow Mountain Community Church where he serves as senior pastor. These ten messages are conveniently packaged in an accessible audio album.

Study Guide

This 144-page study guide correlates with the messages from the *Everything You Need* series by Dr. Jeremiah. Each lesson provides an outline, an overview, and group and personal application questions for each topic.

DVD Message Presentations

Watch Dr. Jeremiah deliver the *Everything You Need* original messages in this special DVD collection.

To order these products, call us at 1-800-947-1993
or visit us online at www.DavidJeremiah.org.

New Video Study for Your Church or Small Group

If you've enjoyed this book, now you can go deeper with the companion video Bible study!

In this six-session study, Dr. David Jeremiah helps you apply the principles in *Everything You Need* to your life. This resource includes video notes, group discussion questions, and personal study and reflection materials for in-between sessions.

Study Guide
9780310111832

DVD
9780310111856

Available now at your favorite bookstore,
or streaming video on StudyGateway.com.

New Bible Study Series from Dr. David Jeremiah

The Jeremiah Bible Study Series captures Dr. David Jeremiah's forty-plus years of commitment to teaching the whole Word of God. Each volume contains twelve lessons for individuals and groups to explore what the Bible says, what it meant to the people at the time it was written, and what it means to us today. Out of his lifelong ministry of delivering the unchanging Word of God to an ever-changing world, Dr. Jeremiah has written this Bible-strong study series focused not on causes, current events, or politics, but on the solid truth of Scripture.

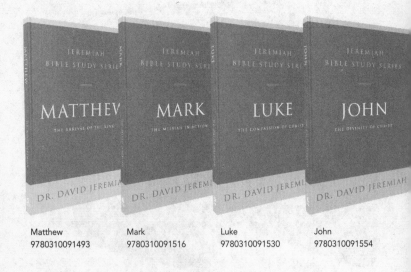

Matthew
9780310091493

Mark
9780310091516

Luke
9780310091530

John
9780310091554

Available now at your favorite bookstore.
More volumes coming soon.

THOMAS NELSON
Since 1798

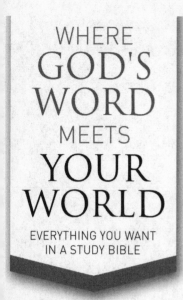
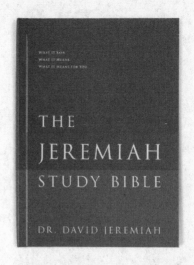

stay connected to the teaching series of

DR. DAVID JEREMIAH

· · · · · · · ·

Publishing | Radio | Television | Online

MORE RESOURCES FROM DR. JEREMIAH

· · · · · · · ·

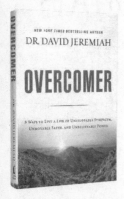

Overcomer

Discover the tools to become an Overcomer in every sense of the word—fully trusting God to prepare you for overcoming the trials and temptations that may cross your path. In this inspiring and practical book, Dr. David Jeremiah uses the armor of God that Paul describes in his letter to the Ephesian church to outline the path to victory.

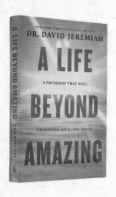

A Life Beyond Amazing

Discouraging headlines, personal adversity, and the toils of daily living often hold us back from living the life God has for us. In *A Life Beyond Amazing*, Dr. David Jeremiah urges us to move past these things, pointing us to a life of blessing beyond our comprehension. He shares nine traits, based on the fruit of the Spirit, that the Church is in need of today, teaching us that God desires for us to live beyond amazing while we await His return.

Stay connected to the teaching ministry of

DAVID JEREMIAH

Publishing | Radio | Television | Online

....

Take advantage of three great ways to let Dr. David Jeremiah give you spiritual direction every day!

Turning Points Magazine and Devotional

Receive Dr. Jeremiah's magazine, *Turning Points*, each month:
- Thematic study focus
- 48 pages of life-changing reading
- Relevant articles
- Daily devotional readings and more!

Request *Turning Points* magazine today!
(800) 947-1993 | DavidJeremiah.org/Magazine

Daily Turning Point E-Devotional

Receive a daily e-devotion from Dr. Jeremiah that will strengthen your walk with God and encourage you to live the authentic Christian life.

Sign up for your free e-devotional today!
www.DavidJeremiah.org/Devo

Turning Point Mobile App

Access Dr. Jeremiah's video teachings, audio sermons, and more . . . whenever and wherever you are!

Download your free app today!
www.DavidJeremiah.org/App

Books Written by David Jeremiah

• • • • • • • • •

- Escape the Coming Night
- Count It All Joy
- The Handwriting on the Wall
- Invasion of Other Gods
- Angels—Who They Are and How They Help…What the Bible Reveals
- The Joy of Encouragement
- Prayer—The Great Adventure
- Overcoming Loneliness
- God in You
- Until Christ Returns
- Stories of Hope
- Slaying the Giants in Your Life
- My Heart's Desire
- Sanctuary
- The Things That Matter
- The Prayer Matrix
- 31 Days to Happiness—Searching for Heaven on Earth
- When Your World Falls Apart
- Turning Points
- Discover Paradise
- Captured by Grace
- Grace Givers
- Why the Nativity?
- Signs of Life
- Life-Changing Moments with God
- Hopeful Parenting
- 1 Minute a Day—Instant Inspiration for the Busy Life
- Grandparenting—Faith That Survives Generations
- In the Words of David Jeremiah
- What in the World Is Going On? The Sovereign and the Suffering
- The 12 Ways of Christmas
- What to Do When You Don't Know What to Do
- Living with Confidence in a Chaotic World
- The Coming Economic Armageddon
- Pathways, Your Daily Walk with God
- What the Bible Says About Love, Marriage, and Sex
- I Never Thought I'd See the Day
- Journey, Your Daily Adventure with God
- The Unchanging Word of God
- God Loves You: He Always Has–He Always Will
- Discovery, Experiencing God's Word Day by Day
- What Are You Afraid Of?
- Destination, Your Journey with God
- Answers to Questions About Heaven
- Answers to Questions About Spiritual Warfare
- Answers to Questions About Adversity
- Answers to Questions About Prophecy
- Quest—Seeking God Daily
- The Upward Call
- Ten Questions Christians are Asking
- Understanding the 66 Books of the Bible
- A.D.—The Revolution That Changed the World
- Agents of the Apocalypse
- Agents of Babylon
- Reset—Ten Steps to Spiritual Renewal
- People Are Asking … Is This the End?
- Hope for Today
- Hope—An Anchor for Life
- 30 Days of Prayer
- Revealing the Mysteries of Heaven
- Greater Purpose
- The God You May Not Know
- Overcomer—8 Ways to Live a Life of Unstoppable Strength, Unmovable Faith, and Unbelievable Power
- The Book of Signs—31 Undeniable Prophecies of the Apocalypse
- In Moments Like These

NEW FROM
DR. DAVID JEREMIAH